Collins

Psychology Research Methods

An Essential Guide

Rachael Thornton

For the IB Diploma Programme

William Collins' dream of knowledge for all began with the publication of his first book in 1819.

A self-educated mill worker, he not only enriched millions of lives, but also founded a flourishing publishing house. Today, staying true to this spirit, Collins books are packed with inspiration, innovation and practical expertise.

They place you at the centre of a world of possibility and give you exactly what you need to explore it.

Published by Collins

An imprint of HarperCollins*Publishers*

The News Building, 1 London Bridge Street, London, SE1 9GF

HarperCollins*Publishers*

Macken House, 39/40 Mayor Street Upper, Dublin 1, D01 C9W8, Ireland

Browse the complete Collins catalogue at

collins.co.uk

Author: Rachael Thornton
Content consultant: Kimberley Croft
Publisher: Catherine Martin
Senior Product Manager: Jennifer Hall
Editorial manager: Michael Chilcott at Haremi
Copyeditor: Carolyn Anderson
Proofreader: Anthony Smith
Permissions researcher: Andrea Collington
Index: LNS Indexing
Cover designer: Amparo Barreras (Kneath Associates)
Cover pattern: SilverCircle/Shutterstock
Typesetter: York Press
Production controller: Alhady Ali
Printed and bound in the UK by Martins the Printers

MIX
Paper | Supporting responsible forestry
FSC™ C013254
www.fsc.org

Acknowledgements

The publishers gratefully acknowledge the permission granted to reproduce the copyright material in this book. Every effort has been made to trace copyright holders and to obtain their permission for the use of copyright material. The publishers will gladly receive any information enabling them to rectify any error or omission at the first opportunity.

We are grateful to the International Baccalaureate Organization for their permission to reproduce copyright material under licence, including Overview diagram of the DP Psychology course framework and key concepts; Tables and guidance on class practicals in the DP Psychology course; Specimen examination questions and related assessment guidance; Associated mark schemes and level descriptors for examination questions; Guidance on interpreting and analysing research data and sources; Internal assessment (IA) criteria for the DP Psychology research report (Criteria A–D); Guidance on research methodology and research considerations within the DP Psychology course; "IB" Wordmark: on front cover, lower right and imprint page © International Baccalaureate Organization, 2025.

This work has been developed independently from and is not endorsed by the International Baccalaureate Organization (IB). International Baccalaureate, Baccalauréat International, Bachillerato Internacional and IB are registered trademarks owned by the International Baccalaureate Organization.

Braun, V. and Clarke, V. (2006). Using thematic analysis in psychology. *Qualitative Research in Psychology,* 3(2), 77–101. https://doi. org/10.1191/1478088706qp063oa Reprinted by permission of the publisher (Taylor & Francis Ltd, http://www. tandfonline.com).

Table of contents

1 Introduction

In IB Psychology, understanding how research is conducted is just as important as understanding what research has found. Research methods form the backbone of the subject – they enable psychologists to investigate behaviour scientifically, evaluate evidence critically, and draw conclusions that are both valid and ethical. Mastering research methods will strengthen your critical thinking skills and help you approach psychological inquiry with confidence.

This book is designed to support you in thinking like a psychologist – a skill that will serve you well in your IB assessments and beyond. It provides a clear, practical approach to understanding the research methods you will use in the class practicals.

A key change in the new IB DP Psychology curriculum is the introduction of class practicals. These allow you to gain hands-on experience of different research methods, including surveys, questionnaires, experiments, interviews and observations. They provide you with different experiences of sampling techniques, data collection and data analysis.

Class practicals are at the heart of the new IB DP Psychology course. They allow you to explore key concepts and content by investigating human behaviour in real-world contexts (**Figure 1.1**).

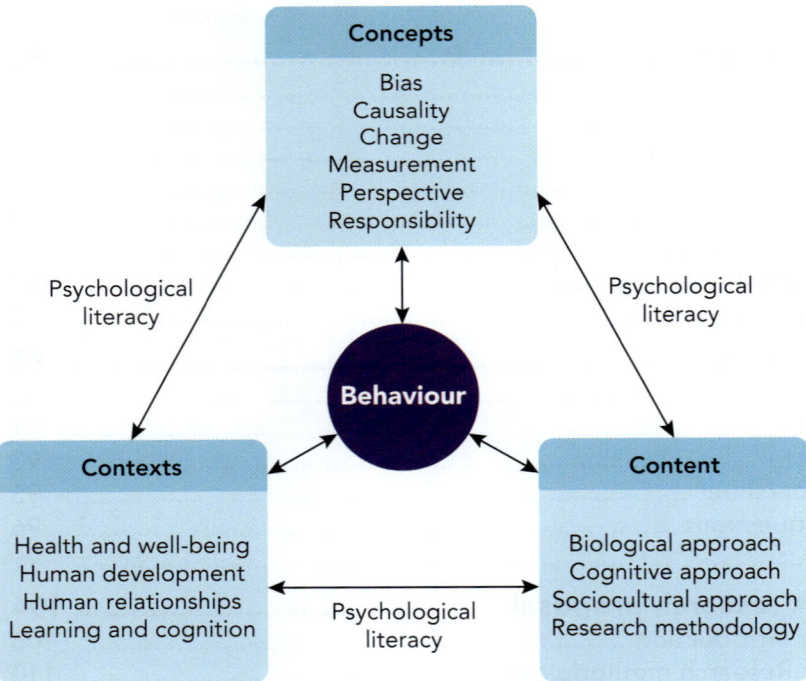

Figure 1.1: *An overview of the IB DP Psychology course*

Each research method is linked to a psychological context (**Table 1.1**). Each chapter in this book provides guidance on planning, conducting and evaluating your research, to help you prepare for Paper 2 in the assessment.

Chapter	Research method	Context
2	Survey/questionnaire	Human relationships
3	Experiment	Learning and cognition
4	Interview/focus group	Health and well-being
5	Observation	Human development

Table 1.1: Research methods and their associated psychological contexts

In the IB DP Psychology course, you are expected to be familiar with data analysis and interpretation. For this reason, each chapter includes a dedicated data analysis and interpretation section. Standard level (SL) students will not be assessed on these skills. However, higher level (HL) students will be expected to use these skills to be successful in Paper 3 of the assessment.

Each chapter also includes an exam-style question and model answer, followed by a practice section for you to apply your knowledge. These questions are ideal for your own individual study, or to discuss with your peers and teacher, in preparation for your assessment.

The final chapter is dedicated to the internal assessment (IA). The IA is an integral part of the course, enabling you to apply the skills and knowledge you have acquired in the class practicals. Chapter 6 provides step-by-step guidance on planning and considerations for the final research proposal that you will submit for internal assessment.

1.1 How to use this book

Key concepts

A table at the start of each chapter explains how the concepts in IB DP Psychology (**Table 1.2**) can be applied to the planning of the practical.

Concept	Explanation
Bias	Bias refers to a deviation from objective thinking, often resulting from an individual's prior experiences, preferences or cultural influences. In psychological research, it is essential to recognise that bias can affect every stage of the research process – from the formulation of a question to the interpretation and publication of results. Common forms include **researcher bias**, **participant bias**, **sampling bias**, **confirmation bias** and **publication bias**.
Causality	Causality refers to the idea that one variable directly influences or causes a change in another, which is known as a cause-and-effect relationship. However, because human behaviour is complex, it is rarely the result of a single factor, which is often thought of as a **reductionist** approach.
Change	Change can be gradual or sudden, planned or unplanned, and influenced by motivation, biology or environmental shifts. Psychologists study how individuals and groups adapt and how to encourage positive change, such as reducing stress or improving health. They also consider resistance to change and assess the effectiveness of interventions at individual, local and global levels.

Concept	Explanation
Measurement	Measurement depends on context, the theory used and how variables are **operationalised**. Psychologists must choose appropriate methods and often use **triangulation** to strengthen the credibility of findings.
Perspective	A perspective refers to a theoretical approach or framework used to understand and explain human behaviour. Each perspective is based on certain assumptions about how and why people think, feel and act, and guides how psychologists conduct research and interpret findings. In IBDP Psychology, you will learn three theoretical perspectives: biological, cognitive and sociocultural.
Responsibility	Psychologists rely on human participants and must treat them with respect, recognising the power they may hold as researchers or professionals. Ethical principles help ensure that benefits outweigh costs, both in human and animal research. Responsibility will be addressed in each chapter when discussing ethical considerations.

Table 1.2: The six key concepts in the study of IB DP Psychology

Features of this book

The book has some key features to support your learning. These include:

- **Key concept box** – These appear at the start of each chapter. They focus on one of the six key concepts and draw out a topic-specific application of this concept.

- **Study in focus box** – These summarise a real-life published example of the research method, helping you to understand how it can work in practice.

- **Activity box** – These activities help to test your knowledge and understanding. They involve either a practical activity or a set of questions to complete, relating to the research method.

- **Compare and contrast it! Table** – These compare the focus research method with the other three research methods.

- **Key terms / Glossary** – These identify commonly used terminology in psychology. At the end of the book, there is an alphabetical glossary of the key terms.

- **Reflection activity box** – These pose a reflective question related to the research method.

- **Class practical planning worksheet** – These worksheets are tailored to the research method. Each chapter includes a model, and a downloadable version is available for you to use.

- **Apply it! Paper 2 practice questions** – Fully worked exam-style questions are provided for each research method, to familiarise you with the Paper 2 assessment. There are also sample questions for you to attempt.

- **Apply it! HL focus** – Fully worked exam-style questions are provided for each research method, to familiarise you with the Paper 3 assessment. There are also sample questions for you to attempt.

- **Answers** – Answers to all practice questions are collated at the end of the book.

1.2 Planning and conducting your class practicals

Research methods you need to know

The IB DP Psychology course is structured around four contexts: human relationships, learning and cognition, health and well-being, and human development. In each context, you will carry out a class practical using a different research method. By the end of the course, you will have completed four compulsory class practicals (**Table 1.3**). You can choose to do more if you wish.

Chapter in book	Context	Research method	Minimum sample size (participants)	Quantitative or qualitative
2	Human relationships	Survey/questionnaire	10	Both
3	Learning and cognition	Experiment (true or quasi-)	5	Quantitative
4	Health and well-being	Interview (structured, semi-structured or focus group)	1 in an interview 3–8 in a focus group	Qualitative
5	Human development	Observation (naturalistic or controlled, overt or covert, participant or non-participant)	1	Can be either qualitative or quantitative

Table 1.3: Class practicals to be conducted within each context

You can conduct a class practical at the start of a context to explore ideas and generate discussion, or at the end to consolidate learning. The IB states a minimum sample size for each practical.

Research methods are generally categorised into **quantitative** and **qualitative** in terms of the type of data collected.

- Quantitative methods collect and analyse numerical data to make inferences about behaviour based on a tested hypothesis. Quantitative data usually has a greater degree of standardisation, which means findings are often more reliable, with the goal of generalising the findings beyond the study.

- Qualitative methods gather textual and verbal data to understand the meanings behind a person's behaviour. In qualitative methods, the focus is more on ensuring the findings have credibility and **transferability** to other settings.

In addition to the research methods you will apply in Chapters 2–5, you need to be aware of two further research methods used by psychologists: **case studies** and **correlational studies**. You could be asked about these in Paper 2.

Case studies

A case study is an in-depth investigation of an individual, group or specific behaviour in a real-life context. It often employs triangulation, meaning researchers use more than one method to gain insight into the behaviour being studied. It is often used when studying rare or unusual behaviours (for example brain damage) or when a behaviour is studied in a natural environment, which makes an experiment unethical.

There are strengths and limitations to case studies:

- **Strengths**: They provide rich, unique insights into specific cases and are often high in ecological validity, as the behaviours take place in a natural setting.
- **Limitations**: They are often based on small or single samples, meaning findings may not be generalisable.

Correlational studies

A correlational study is a quantitative study. It measures the relationship between two variables and whether the relationship is a positive correlation (same direction) or a negative correlation (moving in separate directions). You will explore correlation coefficients in Chapter 2.

There are strengths and limitations to correlational studies:

- **Strengths**: They are often used when it is not practical or ethical to manipulate variables or to explore a relationship to allow further research.
- **Limitations**: A cause-and-effect relationship cannot be established, as there may be other variables affecting the relationship.

Assessing the quality of research

Research methods are the tools of data collection and analysis that allow psychologists to study human behaviour. When planning your class practical, it is important to understand the key ways in which researchers can assess the quality of research findings.

Reliability

Reliability refers to the consistency and dependability of a study or measure. For example, if the study is repeated under the same conditions, it should get the same results. Types of reliability include:

- **Test-retest reliability**: Would you get the same results if you repeated the test at another time? For example, if you gave the same survey to the same set of participants two weeks apart, would the results of the test and retest be consistent?
- **Inter-rater reliability**: Do different researchers agree on the results? For example, when analysing interviews, do the researchers identify the same themes?

Validity

Validity refers to how well a study or tool measures what is intended to be measured. High validity means the research is accurate and applicable. There are three main ways of assessing the validity of research (**Table 1.4**).

Validity in measurement	Face validity: Does the test look like it measures the right thing?	
	Content validity: Does it cover all parts of the concept?	
	Construct validity: Is the tool a truthful measure of the psychological concept?	
Internal validity	The extent to which the independent variable (IV) caused changes in the dependent variable (DV). This causality is often dependent on the level of control of other variables.	
External validity	The extent to which findings can be generalised beyond the study. This can be divided into:	Population validity: Can the results apply to the wider population? This depends on the nature of the sample.
		Ecological validity: Do the results apply to real-life settings? This depends on how natural or artificial the study context is.
		Temporal validity: To what extent can the findings be applied in different time periods? This depends on whether the research is still applicable in contemporary contexts, or if changes in societal norms or knowledge have made the findings outdated.

Table 1.4: *Types of validity in research*

Studies with high internal validity often take place in highly controlled settings, which lowers the ecological validity, which affects the **generalisability**!

Credibility

Credibility refers to how believable and trustworthy a study's findings are. It's a term often used in qualitative research, where traditional measures such as reliability and internal validity can be difficult to apply.

Credibility can be improved by considering **reflexivity**, a process of thinking about how your own background, beliefs or expectations might affect the study. This is especially important in qualitative research, where the researcher is directly involved in data collection and interpretation. Triangulation is a method that involves using more than one researcher, source of data or data collection method to validate findings, thereby improving their credibility.

Sampling techniques

While the IB states the minimum number of participants (see Table 1.4), an important consideration is deciding who and how you will obtain your sample. **Sampling** is the process of obtaining participants from the group of people being studied, known as the **population of interest** (or target population). It is very rare that a researcher can study everyone in the target population. Therefore, they try to find a sample that is **representative** of the diversity of those in the wider population. The source from which the sample is drawn is known as the **sampling frame**. For example, a list of telephone numbers could provide a sample frame for telephone surveys.

There are two distinct types of sampling:

- **Probability sampling**, in which everyone in the target population has a chance of being chosen.
- **Non-probability sampling**, in which participants are selected or purposefully chosen.

Broadly speaking, probability methods tend to be more representative of the population of interest. This means that the findings have greater population validity. In turn, this means the findings can be applied to a wider population.

Psychology research is often criticised for having sampling bias, especially when the sample consists primarily of university students. This is because university students are often WEIRD: Western, Educated, Industrialised, Rich and Democratic, making them unrepresentative of the wider global population.

Table 1.5 describes different sampling techniques, and their strengths and limitations.

Sampling technique	Description	Quantitative or qualitative	Probability or non-probability	Strengths	Limitations
Random	Each member of the population has an equal chance of being selected, using a random-number generator or lottery method.	Quantitative	Probability	<ul><li>Unbiased, as everyone has the same chance of being chosen</li><li>Representative, if the sample is large enough</li></ul>	<ul><li>Reliant on a sample frame to choose the population from</li><li>The element of chance can lead to the sample not being representative</li></ul>
Stratified	The target population is divided into subgroups. Participants are then drawn from each subgroup.	Quantitative	Probability	<ul><li>Very representative, as subgroups are included proportionately</li></ul>	<ul><li>Time-consuming</li><li>Reliant on having knowledge of the subgroups to include</li></ul>
Opportunity	Participants are selected based on who is readily available to take part.	Both	Non-probability	<ul><li>Quick and easy to find participants</li><li>Often cost-effective</li></ul>	<ul><li>Can be less representative of the target population as it is based upon availability</li><li>Prone to sampling bias</li></ul>

Sampling technique	Description	Quantitative or qualitative	Probability or non-probability	Strengths	Limitations
Self-selected	Often known as volunteer sampling, participants agree to take part, usually by responding to an advertisement.	Both In qualitative research, there may be exclusion criteria.	Non-probability	• Participants are often highly motivated to take part	• May lead to a biased sample as only those interested or who feel confident may volunteer • This means not all types of participants are represented
Snowball	Existing participants recruit other participants. This technique is often used to study hard-to-reach groups or where there is no sample frame.	Qualitative	Non-probability	• Useful for studying hidden or hard-to-reach target populations	• Risk of sampling bias • May end up with a sample with similar characteristics

Table 1.5: Different sampling techniques

Activity 1: Practising sampling

1. Read the statements. Identify which sampling technique was used in each case.

   a. A psychology student puts up posters around their university campus asking students to take part in a study on sleep and stress.

   b. A student walks into the school's student common area and asks the first 15 people they see to fill in a questionnaire on exercise.

   c. A study on nicotine addiction starts by interviewing one person from a support group. This person helps the researcher connect with four other people they know who have also experienced addiction.

   d. A student is provided with a list of the 200 students in their school. They use a random generator to select 30 students for a memory and music experiment.

   e. A psychologist wants to study attitudes towards mental health across different age groups. They divide the population into three age groups (adolescents, working-age adults and retired older adults) and randomly select people from each group in proportion to its share of the total population.

2. Psychology research is often criticised for having sampling bias, especially when the sample consists primarily of university students. This is because university students are often WEIRD: Western, Educated, Industrialised, Rich and Democratic, making them unrepresentative of the wider global population. For each of the samples in a, b and d in question 1, identify **one** reason why a student-only sample could bias the findings.

Research process

You will use a worksheet to plan each class practical in context. The **Class practical planning worksheet** can be found at the end of each method's chapter (2–5). Your teacher needs to approve your plan before you begin the research.

Figure 1.2 shows the basic steps of psychological research that you will follow in each class practical.

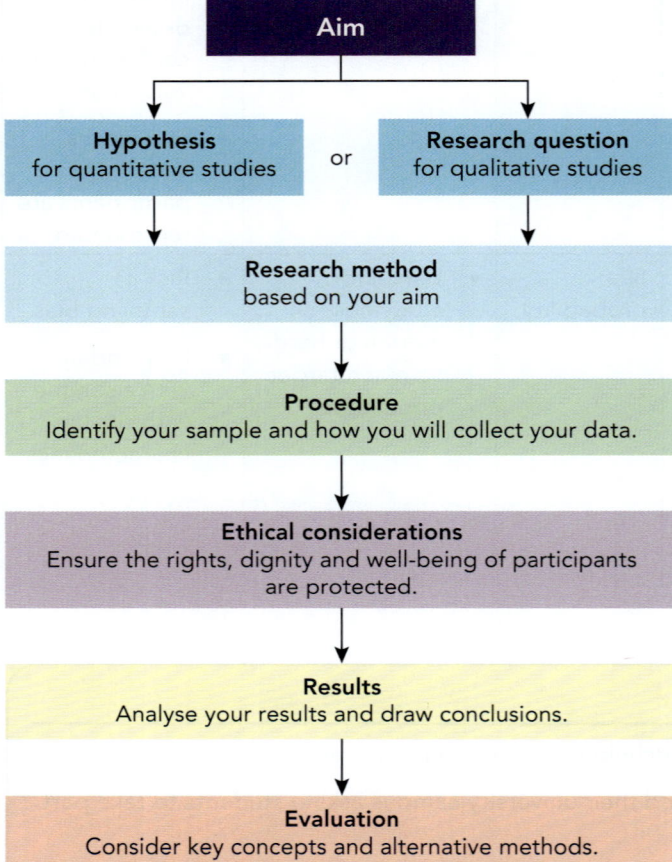

Figure 1.2: *Basic steps in psychological research*

The key to a good practical is to consider the aim of your study – that is, what you intend to investigate or examine. The goals of qualitative and quantitative research are often different. For example, on the topic of whether listening to music is useful when studying, the aims might be as follows.

- With quantitative research, the goal is usually to assess the impact or effect.

  Aim: *To investigate whether listening to music affects IB students' serial recall.*

- With qualitative research, the goal is usually to explore attitudes and perceptions.

  Aim: *To explore IB students' perceptions of listening to music while studying.*

Note that in both cases the aim is specific. Ensure your aim is specific.

When you evaluate your study, think of it in terms of key concepts (refer to **Table 1.2**) and what alternative methods you could use. Use the **Class practical recording sheet** to review your class practical. This is mapped to the questions in Paper 2, providing you with a useful revision resource. The *Class practical recording sheet* can be downloaded from collins.co.uk/internationalresources.

The template for the *Class practical recording sheet* can be re-used for every context. Keep copies in your revision folder.

Paper 2: Class practical recording sheet

Q1a. Aim and design: What was the purpose of the class practical? What was your research method and subtype? Who was in your sample?

Q1a. Procedure: Explain how you carried out the class practical, including any materials, controls and considerations taken.

Q1b. Application: You need to apply **one** of the key concepts to your class practical. You should practise all of them:		
Bias: What did you do to control for biases? What biases might still be present?	**Causality:** How far can you make conclusions about cause and effect?	**Change:** How does the study measure change over time?
Measurement: How far were the tools or questions reliable and valid?	**Perspective:** How far did you include alternate perspectives?	**Responsibility:** Which ethical considerations were important in the study?

Q1c. Compare and contrast: How could your class practical be compared to any of the other research methods listed in the IB DP specification, including: experiments, observations, surveys/questionnaires, interviews or focus groups, correlational studies, or case studies? Ensure that you feel confident discussing any similarities or differences in detail.

Q1d. Design: How could you design the same study using **one** of the following methods: survey/questionnaire, experiment, interview, observation, correlational study or case study?

HL

HL Paper 3 Q2 Data analysis: Summarise the type of data analysis used. What conclusions can be drawn?

HL Paper 3 Q3 Research considerations: How could you evaluate your practical in terms of credibility, bias and transferability?

In your revision, practise rotating methods. For example, if your class practical used an interview, be ready to:

- compare it with an experiment
- design an observation on the same topic.

1.3 Ethical considerations in class practicals
Responsibility

One of the key concepts in the new curriculum is the concept of responsibility. This emphasises the role of researchers in making reasoned and responsible decisions regarding the conduct and reporting of research. In animal research, this is to ensure the level of harm is minimised. In terms of your research, you will be considering the rights and dignity of human participants.

Before conducting any class practical, your plan, along with ethical considerations, must be approved by your teacher. The IB follows the same ethical guidelines as organisations such as the British Psychological Society (BPS), American Psychological Association (APA) and Indian Psychological Association (IPA), which are:

- **Informed consent**: All participants need to voluntarily agree to take part in your study and sign the *Participant consent form*. According to the IB, if participants are under 16 years old, you need to obtain the written consent of the parent(s) or guardian(s). When you conduct a class practical in school, you must also obtain the written consent of the relevant teachers.

- **Confidentiality**: This refers to keeping participants' data private and ensuring that only the researchers know their identity.

- **Anonymity**: You should not collect and share any names or identifying information about participants.

- **Right to withdraw**: During consent, you must inform participants that they can leave the study and/or remove their data at any time.

- **Deception**: You should avoid deceiving participants. However, slight deception by omission can be important in experiments, but it must not cause harm and you should discuss it in the debrief.

- **Protection from harm**: There should be no undue stress, physical harm or stigmatisation of participants. Class practicals should always be supervised by a teacher and ethical guidelines should be adhered to.

- **Debrief**: You should share the aims of your research after data collection, and provide any necessary support or aftercare.

Not allowed for class practicals

In your class practical, you *cannot* undertake animal research, conformity, or obedience studies. Naturalistic observations must also be in public spaces.

Study in Focus

Bandura (1961): Do children imitate aggression?

Albert Bandura conducted a classic study on whether children learn behaviour through observation and imitation of adult models. In the experiment, 72 children (aged 3–6 years) were assigned to one of three conditions:

- observing an aggressive adult model who physically and verbally attacked an inflatable Bobo doll

- a non-aggressive model who quietly played with toys

- no model (the control group).

Baseline aggression data was gathered from parents and teachers to match the children across groups to control for individual differences. After observing the models, children were deliberately frustrated – they were denied access to attractive toys. They were then left in a room with the Bobo doll, while their behaviours were observed through a one-way mirror.

The study found that children who saw the aggressive model were more likely to reproduce physical and verbal aggression, demonstrating that behaviour can be learned through observation and imitation.

This experiment supported Bandura's social learning theory, arguing that humans learn behaviours through observing and imitating others.

Reflection questions

1. What ethical considerations are raised in Bandura's study?

2. To what extent do you think exposure to aggression had long-term effects on the children's behaviour? Explain your answer.

3. Would Bandura's experiment be approved by an ethics committee today? Why? Why not?

Bandura, A., Ross, D, and Ross, S. A. (1961). Transmission of aggression through imitation of aggressive models. *The Journal of Abnormal and Social Psychology, 63*(3), 575.

The following forms are intended to be used when undertaking a class practical to ensure you give informed consent and debrief participants at the end. These can be edited for your class practical, but provide a structure to follow to be a responsible researcher. *Remember that class practicals must not involve deception, distressing topics, or studies on conformity and obedience.*

Debrief script

Dear Participant,

Thank you for taking part in our psychology research. This debrief provides a short overview of the study's aim, background and expected findings.

We aimed to investigate: *(Insert aim – for example, whether the wording in a question influenced recall.)*

The theory behind the study was: *(Explain the theory/studies on which it is based – for example, schema theory.)*

Based on this, we expected to find: *(What did you expect to find? For example, those with context would make greater associations to their schemas, and this would aid recall.)*

Once the analysis is complete, we will be happy to share the results with you.

If you have any questions or would like more information, please contact: *(Insert your name and contact details.)*

Participant consent form

Dear Participant,

Thank you for your interest in joining our psychology research. Please read this form carefully. If at the end you feel comfortable participating, please sign the form.

Aim of the research: *(Insert a clear and simple statement of what the study is about. If you are doing an experiment and do not want the full aim disclosed, provide the topic – for example, a study on recall of letters.)*

What you will be asked to do: *(Briefly explain the procedure/ process to the participant.)*

Your rights as a participant:

- Your identity will remain anonymous and your personal data will remain confidential.
- You may withdraw yourself and your data at any time.
- Any materials, transcripts or recordings will be destroyed after the research has concluded.
- The findings will be shared with you after the results have been analysed.

If you have any questions at any time, please contact: *(Add your email.)*

By signing this form, I have read and understood the information above, and I agree to take part in the study.

Participant signature: _____

Date: _____

Parent/guardian signature: _____

Date: _____
(parental/guardian consent required when the participant is younger than 16 years)

These templates can be downloaded from collins.co.uk/internationalresources.

1.4 Requirements for assessment

Paper 2

Paper 2 in the assessment requires you to apply concepts and content to research contexts. It comprises two sections: Section A and Section B.

You are given **1 hour 30 minutes** to complete both sections.

For SL students, Paper 2 forms 35% of your final assessment; for HL students, it forms 25%.

Section A

Suggested time: 50 minutes

Paper 2 Section A comprises four compulsory questions focused on the class practicals that you do in each context.

To score full marks, you must use relevant, method-specific terminology (such as control variables, triangulation, credibility). This depth is what distinguishes a top-band response.

Question 1a. Describe how you used a/an [research method] in your class practical, including the aim and procedure. **(4 marks)**

What is it asking you to do?

You need to demonstrate your knowledge of the method and how you used it in a class practical.

Look back at your *Class practical recording sheet* and the boxes labelled **1a**. Explain the aim and the procedure you used, using accurate key terminology that is relevant to the method.

Note that you will only score a maximum of two marks if you give a generic response and do not explicitly mention how the characteristics of the method link to *your* class practical.

Mark scheme: Knowledge and understanding

Mark	Level descriptor
0	The work does not reach a standard described by the descriptors below.
1–2	• The response demonstrates limited knowledge and understanding of the research methodology relevant to the class practical. • Psychological terminology is limited or contains some inaccuracies.
3–4	• The response demonstrates detailed knowledge and understanding of the research methodology relevant to the class practical. • Psychological terminology is used accurately.

Question 1b. Explain the concept of [one of the six key concepts] in relation to your [same research method in **1a**] class practical. **(4 marks)**

What is it asking you to do?

You need to explain how the concept given is relevant to the class practical you carried out. In some cases, this might involve explaining how you considered and tried to reduce issues linked to the concept (such as bias). In other cases, you might explain how the concept applies.

As you go through the different sections of this book, you will see **Key concept** features. These are designed to help you explore how each of the six concepts relates to your class practical. You can then make these explicit in your *Class practical recording sheet*, showing where you addressed or accounted for the concept and where it remained a limitation.

Remember, the six key concepts are:

- bias
- measurement
- causality
- perspective
- change
- responsibility.

Mark scheme: Application

Mark	Level descriptor
0	The work does not reach a standard described by the descriptors below.
1–2	• The knowledge and understanding of the concept is relevant but limited. • There are some relevant links between the concept and the class practical.
3–4	• The knowledge and understanding of the concept is well developed. • There are clear and detailed links between the concept and the class practical.

Question 1c. Compare and contrast the use of a/an [research method in **1a**] used in your class practical with a/an [a different research method]. **(6 marks)**

What is it asking you to do?

You are being asked to explain the similarities and differences between your class practical and the research method provided.

Write two distinct paragraphs: one explaining the similarities and one explaining the differences.

At the start of each class practical chapter, there is a table comparing the research method in that context to other research methods. This could be any one of the six methods you will study, which are:

- survey/questionnaire
- experiment
- interview/focus group
- observation
- case study
- correlational study.

Mark scheme: Compare and contrast

Mark	Level descriptor
0	The work does not reach a standard described by the descriptors below.
1–2	• Similarities or differences are described in limited detail or contain errors. • There is limited psychological terminology relevant to the research methods.
3–4	• Similarities and differences are explained in limited detail and may lack clarity or either similarities or differences are discussed in detail. • Psychological terminology relevant to the research methods is used, but with some inaccuracies.
5–6	• Similarities and differences are discussed in detail. • Psychological terminology relevant to the research methods is used effectively.

Question 1d. Design a/an [new research method] to investigate the same topic as you investigated in your class practical. **(6 marks)**

What is it asking you to do?

Design a new practical using the research method given with the same aim and research question as the one in question **1a**.

You need to provide details of how you will select the sample and the procedure you will use, using the correct terminology.

Mark scheme: Design

Mark	Level descriptor
0	The work does not reach a standard described by the descriptors below.
1–2	• The procedure of the research method is described in limited detail or contains inaccuracies. • There is limited use of psychological terminology relevant to the research method.
3–4	• The procedure of the research method is explained in some detail but lacks clarity. • Psychological terminology relevant to the research method is used, but with some inaccuracies.
5–6	• The procedure of the research method is explained with accuracy and detail. • Psychological terminology relevant to the research method is used effectively.

Section B

Suggested time: 40 minutes

Paper 2 Section B comprises a question requiring you to evaluate an unseen research study with regard to two or more concepts.

Question 2. Discuss the following study with reference to two or more of the following concepts: [several of the six key concepts will be listed here]. **(15 marks)**

What is it asking you to do?

You will be given a summary of a study that links to one of the four contexts (human relationships, learning and cognition, health and well-being, or human development). You will then need to choose **at least two** of the listed concepts to discuss. Remember that *discuss* means to suggest ways in which the concept has been considered, or how it could be further considered.

To reach the top mark band, you need to select two or more concepts to discuss. You need to make links between the concepts and source material, as well as use accurate and precise terminology. You need to apply critical analysis with an argument that has a well-reasoned conclusion.

Use the research you learn for Paper 1 to practise this question!

Mark scheme: Evaluation

Mark	Level descriptor
0	The work does not reach a standard described by the descriptors below.
1–3	• The response indicates little understanding of, and critical engagement with, any of the specified concepts in relation to the study. • The response is descriptive. Any analysis present is superficial or incoherent. Links between concepts and source material are not included or are irrelevant to the discussion. Where a conclusion is included, this is very superficial or is not consistent with the rest of the response. • Psychological terminology is not used or is consistently used inappropriately. Points are frequently inaccurate and unclear. There are few, if any, references to the study.
4–6	• The response indicates a basic understanding of, and critical engagement with, at least one of the specified concepts in relation to the study. • There is limited analysis present and overall the response is more descriptive than it is analytical. Links between concepts and the study are of limited relevance or ineffectively support the discussion. A simplistic conclusion is included. • Psychological terminology is used, but often inappropriately. Points are frequently imprecise or vague. There are occasional references to the study.

Mark	Level descriptor
7–9	• The response indicates some understanding of, and critical engagement with, one or more of the specified concepts in relation to the study. • The response contains analysis, although this analysis lacks development. Links between concepts and the source material are relevant, but they lack development in support of the discussion. A conclusion is included. • Psychological terminology is used, sometimes appropriately. Relevant points are made but lack accuracy and development. Specific references to the study are made, although these are sometimes ineffective.
10–12	• The response indicates good understanding of, and critical engagement with, at least two of the specified concepts in relation to the study. • The response contains critical analysis, although this analysis lacks development. Links between concepts and the study are used to support the discussion. The response argues to a conclusion that is consistent with the arguments presented. • Psychological terminology is used, mostly appropriately. Points made are relevant and accurate but lack detail. There are specific references to the study.
13–15	• The response indicates very good understanding of, and critical engagement with, two or more of the specified concepts in relation to the study. • The response contains well-developed critical analysis. Links between concepts and source material are relevant and well developed and effectively support the discussion The response argues to a reasoned and clearly stated conclusion that is consistent with the arguments presented. • There is accurate and precise use of psychological terminology. Points are relevant, accurate and detailed. There are specific and effective references to the study.

Paper 3 (HL focus)

You will *all* study data analysis and interpretation (both SL and HL students), as you will learn core analysis skills. However, **only HL students** will be examined on this as part of their assessment, in Paper 3. Each chapter in this book explains the analysis of each method, which will help you prepare for Paper 3.

Paper 3 duration: 1 hour 45 minutes

Paper 3 comprises four source-based questions requiring you to analyse and interpret research data. The paper forms 30% of your final assessment if you are an HL student.

In the exam, you will be provided with five pieces of research data in a source booklet, featuring both qualitative and quantitative data. This data may be real or fictional. The sources will always link to one of the **HL contexts,** which are:

- technology
- culture
- motivation

and their roles in shaping behaviour. You will find it useful to analyse your class practicals, to help you prepare for Paper 3.

Question 1. Explain **one** issue that limits the interpretation of the data in **Source 1.**

(3 marks)

What is it asking you to do?

Source 1 will always present a graph. You should explain only **one** issue. If you state more than one, you will be marked on your first point. The key is to provide an explanation of *why* the issue prevents the data from being interpreted.

Mark scheme: Interpretation of graphs

Mark	Level descriptor
0	The work does not reach a standard described by the descriptors below.
1	A relevant issue is identified.
2	A relevant issue is clearly described.
3	A relevant issue is explained.

Question 2. Analyse the findings from **Source 2** and state a conclusion linked to the claim [topic will link to a HL context]. **(6 marks)**

What is it asking you to do?

Aim to analyse the findings from **Source 2** in detail, and state a conclusion explicitly linked to the findings.

Mark scheme: Data analysis

Mark	Level descriptor
0	The work does not reach a standard described by the descriptors below.
1–2	• There is limited analysis of the data or the analysis contains inaccuracies. • A conclusion is attempted but it is not relevant.
3–4	• Analysis of the data is accurate but lacks detail or development. • A conclusion is stated but the link to the findings lacks clarity.
5–6	• The data is analysed in detail. • A conclusion is stated that is explicitly linked to the findings.

Question 3. **One** of three possible evaluation questions for qualitative data will be asked about **Source 3**. The question is worth **6 marks**.

- Discuss how the researcher could improve the credibility of the findings.
- *OR* Discuss how the researcher could avoid bias.
- *OR* Discuss to what extent the findings are transferable to other populations or contexts.

What is it asking you to do?

You need to offer a considered and balanced review that includes a range of factors. Support your conclusions using evidence from the source; do not simply paraphrase. Ensure you use accurate and precise terminology.

Mark scheme: Research considerations

Mark	Level descriptor
0	The work does not reach a standard described by the descriptors below.
1–2	• Discussion shows limited understanding of the research consideration. • Reference to relevant supporting evidence from the source is limited or missing.
3–4	• Discussion shows some understanding of the research consideration, but with some inaccuracies. • Reference to relevant supporting evidence from the source is implicit.
5–6	• Discussion shows detailed understanding of the research consideration. • Reference to the relevant supporting evidence from the source is explicit.

Question 4. To what extent can we conclude [claim of the sources shown]? In your answer, use your own knowledge and **at least three** of **Sources 2–5**.

(15 marks)

What is it asking you to do?

To what extent means you need to interpret the data from at least three of the given sources, and use your knowledge to present ways in which the claim is and is not supported (that is, its validity).

To get into the top mark band, you need to:

- clearly answer the question using detailed and well-developed knowledge from the HL extension areas (culture, technology, motivation)
- critically analyse at least three sources, applying relevant research methods to support your argument.
- compare the sources effectively and evaluate how they support or challenge the claim.
- write a clear, reasoned conclusion that is fully supported by your analysis.

Mark scheme: Synthesis

Mark	Level descriptor
0	The work does not reach a standard described by the descriptors below.
1–3	• The response indicates little understanding of the demands of the question. Knowledge and understanding relevant to the claim are anecdotal or of very marginal relevance. • The response is mostly descriptive. Any analysis present is superficial or incoherent. Knowledge relevant to one or more of the sources is included but there is no clear link to the claim. • There is little or no discussion of different points of view. Where a conclusion is included, it is superficial or is not consistent with the rest of the response.

Mark	Level descriptor
4–6	• The response indicates some understanding of the demands of the question. Knowledge and understanding relevant to the claim are limited or of marginal relevance. There is limited discussion of the extent to which the claim is valid. • The response contains limited analysis and overall is more descriptive than analytical. Relevant knowledge is used to interpret one or more of the sources but with inaccuracies or without a clear link to the claim. • There is little relevant discussion of different points of view. A simplistic conclusion is included.
7–9	• The response indicates understanding of the demands of the question, but these demands are only partially addressed. Knowledge and understanding relevant to the claim are limited or lack clarity. There is some discussion of the extent to which the claim is valid. • The response contains analysis, although this analysis lacks development. Relevant knowledge is used to interpret at least two of the sources but the link to the claim is limited. • There is some discussion on relevant and different points of view. The response includes a conclusion that is only partially supported by evidence.
10–12	• The demands of the question are understood and addressed. Knowledge and understanding relevant to the claim have some detail with some development. There is discussion of the extent to which the claim is valid, but the response lacks some detail. • The response contains critical analysis, although this analysis lacks development. Relevant knowledge is used to interpret two or more of the sources to support the discussion of the claim. • There is some discussion of different points of view. The response argues to a conclusion that is consistent with the arguments presented.
13–15	• The demands of the question are understood and addressed. Knowledge and understanding relevant to the claim are detailed and well developed. There is detailed relevant discussion of the extent to which the claim is valid. • The response contains well-developed critical analysis. Relevant knowledge is used to interpret at least three of the sources and is used effectively to support the discussion of the claim. • Different points of view are identified and evaluated. The response argues to a reasoned and clearly stated conclusion that is consistent with the arguments presented.

Internal assessment (IA) research proposal

IA duration: 20 hours

Your IA is internally assessed by your teacher and externally moderated.

For SL students, the IA forms 30% of your final assessment; for HL students, it forms 20%.

For your IA, you need to write a research proposal using one of the research methods from your class practicals, which are:

- survey/questionnaire
- experiment (true or quasi-)
- interview (structured, semi-structured or focus group)
- observation (naturalistic or controlled, overt or covert, participant or non-participant).

Through undertaking your four class practicals, you will build the skills and confidence you need to design your own psychological study. In each section of your research proposal, you will demonstrate the skills you have learned:

1. **Introduction** → Develop a clear aim and research question or hypothesis.

2. **Methodology** → Choose an appropriate research method and sampling technique, and review ethical and procedural considerations.

3. **Data collection** → Construct tools to collect data and understand the challenges in data collection.

4. **Evaluation** → Reflect on the strengths, limitations and implications of your collected data.

The structure needed for the write-up of your research proposal is the same as the assessment criteria. You will find out more about this in Chapter 6 of this book, where the assessment criteria are discussed in detail.

Your IA is an exciting way to explore topics in which you are interested, and apply psychology to the real world!

Human relationships: Surveys and questionnaires

For the context Human relationships, you need to be able to conduct a **survey** or a **questionnaire** with a minimum of 10 participants.

There are a few differences between a survey and a questionnaire:

- Surveys refer to the entire research process, including the design of the questions, their distribution to participants and the analysis of the data.

- A questionnaire is a data collection tool that consists of a written set of questions to explore participants' thoughts and experiences, often using **open-ended questions** as part of other methods, such as interviews.

However, in your IB DP Psychology course, you are not expected to distinguish between surveys and questionnaires. Instead, you can use the terms interchangeably. In this book, the term 'surveys' is used.

You can apply the key concepts in **Table 2.1** to surveys.

Concept	Application
Change	The survey design you choose will influence how well you can study change. Most surveys only look at a human behaviour at one point in time.
Measurement	The measurement of a survey depends on clear **operationalisation** – for example, clearly defining the variables and stating how you will measure them. It also depends on an appropriate scale design, which refers to how response options are structured to measure participants' attitudes or behaviours.
Perspective	The way in which survey questions are framed often reflects certain psychological perspectives in terms of the researchers, the approach and the participants.
Bias	Surveys are prone to various biases, which can distort findings. You must consider any possible biases when you design your survey and interpret the data.
Causality	You can draw correlations from surveys, but they cannot show causality.
Responsibility	Psychologists have a responsibility to design ethical surveys that respect participants' rights when asking questions about relationships.

Table 2.1: The six key concepts and their application to surveys

2.1 Introduction to surveys and questionnaires

What are surveys?

A survey is a time-efficient method that allows researchers to collect data from large groups, often using **self-report** techniques, in which participants provide information about their own thoughts, feelings or behaviours. Surveys involve answering pre-determined questions and are widely used due to their flexibility – they can include both open-ended questions, which produce **qualitative** data, and **closed-ended questions**, which generate **quantitative** data. They can also be administered in various formats, such as face to face, online, by post or over the phone, making them a versatile research method.

Surveys can cover different time spans:

- **Cross-sectional** surveys provide a snapshot of behaviour at one point in time; they cannot capture development or changes over time.
- **Longitudinal** surveys are designed to track the same participants over time, allowing researchers to observe patterns of change.

Surveys are useful in studying human relationships as the topics often involve personal experiences, which cannot be observed directly and may not be ethical to manipulate. The anonymity of self-reporting responses can often, therefore, increase participation and **validity**.

Study in focus

Yuki (2003): Does culture influence how we form group identity?

Yuki (2003) investigated how North American and East Asian individuals conceptualise group identity. Participants were students (126 American and 122 Japanese) who answered questions about a small in-group (for example a club) and a large in-group (their country) with which they identified. They rated statements on a six-point scale measuring loyalty, group identity, knowledge of relationships within the group, similarity between members and group status.

Japanese students felt closer to small groups, demonstrating understanding of the personal ties between members. American students identified more with large groups with shared values, viewing group identity based on shared characteristics or social categories. The study shows cultural differences in how group identity is formed and understood.

Reflection

1. What are the strengths and limitations of using surveys to study cultural differences in group behaviour?
2. How might social desirability bias affect participants' responses in surveys about group identity and social relationships?
3. Was Yuki's (2003) approach inductive or deductive? Why?

Yuki, M. (2003). Intergroup comparison versus intragroup relationships: A cross-cultural examination of social identity theory in North American and East Asian cultural contexts. *Social Psychology Quarterly*, 166–183.

Key concept: Perspective

Positivists typically take a deductive approach. They begin with a theory or hypothesis and use research methods, such as surveys, to test whether the data support it. **Interpretivists**, on the other hand, take an inductive approach, using surveys to generate qualitative research to interpret meaning from participants' responses to generate a theory.

Key concept: Bias

It is possible to reduce **social desirability bias**, in which people may respond in a socially acceptable way rather than truthfully, by using anonymity.

Using neutral wording in questions helps avoid leading question bias, in which participants are influenced toward a specific answer, and **acquiescence bias**, where they tend to agree with statements even if they don't fully believe them.

As surveys rely on self-reported data, there is an element of **recall bias**, in which responses are reliant on memory. Comparing findings from surveys with other methods is a way to increase the **credibility**, ensuring responses reflect the participants' actual experiences.

Survey design

Human relationships often involve measuring abstract concepts, such as attraction, with surveys turning them into questions and numerical responses. This process requires careful design to ensure that what is measured is both accurate and consistent. Having each question target one psychological construct will help improve the precision of the measurement and improve **construct validity**.

When researchers study human relationships, they often use **Likert scales**, in which participants rate how strongly they agree with statements on a scale (for example from strongly agree to strongly disagree). Using clear language and standardised response scales increases **reliability** by reducing misunderstanding and inconsistency. Often, the scale includes a neutral midpoint to allow for neutral attitudes. However, some researchers argue that its inclusion can lead to responses given with little cognitive effort.

Researchers sometimes use cognitive speed bumps – techniques that slow down the respondent's thinking to improve the thoughtfulness and reliability of their responses. This could include removing the neutral option, reordering the scale (by having the second question reverse the scale), rephrasing the question or adding follow-up questions.

Reflection activity

Imagine you are designing a 10-question survey on factors that lead to conflict in romantic relationships, to distribute to a sample of busy teachers. You want to gather honest, valid data.

1. Why might including a neutral midpoint on your Likert scale be a limitation?

2. How could cognitive speed bumps (for example reversed items, varied phrasing) be useful here?

Responsibility: Being an ethical researcher

In line with IB ethical guidelines for psychology, researchers need to consider the following points for studies into human relationships.

- **No studies on conformity or obedience**: Even when you conduct a study using a survey, it is important to choose topics that avoid inducing distress or peer pressure.

- **Confidentiality and anonymity**: You must make it clear to participants how you will protect their data. You will not share their responses with others and you will keep their identities private (confidentiality). Anonymity goes a step further – you should not collect any identifying information, so responses cannot be linked back to individuals. These safeguards help participants feel safe to respond honestly, which is especially important in school-based research in which participants may know one another.

- **Protection from harm**: In your class practicals, you must avoid distressing or sensitive topics. It is also important to carefully design your questions to avoid harm and ensure they are not leading, biased or judgmental. Ask a classmate to review your questions or pilot them with your class to get feedback. Be mindful and respectful of the diversity of human experiences and relationships – avoid making assumptions about participants' backgrounds or identities.

- **Voluntary participation**: Ensure participants understand that their involvement is entirely voluntary. They should not feel pressured to take part or to answer every question. You must inform participants that they can skip any items or withdraw their data at any time without penalty. This protects their well-being and autonomy, allowing them to remain in control of their participation throughout.

Compare and contrast It!: Paper 2 Question 1c

Surveys versus other research methods

Paper 2 Section A Question **1c** will ask you to compare and contrast your survey with another research method. Use **Table 2.2** to help plan your response. Remember that in the exam you will need to discuss each similarity and difference in detail. For example:

Surveys are useful for collecting data from large samples, which increases generalisability. In contrast, experiments often involve smaller samples due to practical constraints, which can limit external validity. This reflects different assumptions about how psychological knowledge is generated. While surveys prioritise breadth, experiments focus on internal validity.

Similarities	Differences
Surveys vs interviews	
• Both can generate qualitative data and can use member checking in which researchers ask participants to review and clarify their interpretation. This enhances credibility. • Both are self-report techniques that can investigate relationships but not establish causality. • Both may include standardised questions. **Structured interviews** follow an interview guide, while surveys use fixed, pre-written items. For more information on interviews, see Chapter 4.	• Surveys are typically completed independently, whereas interviews involve direct interaction with a researcher, increasing the risk of interviewer or **researcher bias**. • Surveys are structured and standardised, whereas **semi-structured interviews** involve flexibility based on participants' responses. • Surveys are often anonymous, which can reduce social desirability bias. Interviews, especially in **focus groups**, may be influenced by interviewer presence or group dynamics.
Surveys vs experiments	
• Both methods employ a systematic approach to data collection and can be applied to large sample sizes. • Both methods can examine relationships between variables. • Both can be used to test hypotheses and aim to produce findings that are **generalisable** to a wider population. For more information on experiments, see Chapter 3.	• Surveys collect subjective self-reported data, often completed privately, while **experiments** collect objective behavioural data in controlled settings. • Surveys only establish correlation; experiments can identify cause and effect. • Surveys are typically conducted in real-world or naturalistic environments, while experiments are often conducted in controlled laboratory settings.

Similarities	Differences
Surveys vs observations	
<ul><li>Both methods take a structured approach with standardised tools, such as checklists or rating scales.</li><li>Both methods can collect either qualitative or quantitative data, depending on the design.</li><li>Both can be used to explore behaviour, but neither can establish causality.</li></ul>For more information on observations, see Chapter 5.	<ul><li>Surveys gather self-reported data (what participants *say*), whereas **observations** record actual behaviour (what participants *do*).</li><li>Surveys usually measure attitudes or perceptions about behaviour, while observations focus on directly observable actions.</li><li>Surveys are completed by participants, whereas observations are conducted by researchers who record participants' behaviour.</li></ul>
Surveys vs case studies	
<ul><li>Both methods are commonly used in psychology to investigate real-world behaviour through direct or self-reported data from participants.</li><li>Both can produce qualitative data and quantitative data.</li><li>Both are subject to researcher bias and require careful design or **triangulation** to ensure validity and credibility of findings.</li></ul>For more information on case studies, see Chapter 1.	<ul><li>Surveys are used to collect data from large samples to identify patterns or trends across a population, whereas **case studies** focus on one individual or a small group to gain detailed insight.</li><li>Surveys typically use structured, standardised questionnaires with fixed questions; case studies use a combination of methods such as interviews, observations and tests.</li><li>Surveys are often generalisable if sampling is appropriate, while case studies are less generalisable but provide rich, contextual understanding of a behaviour.</li></ul>
Surveys vs correlational studies	
<ul><li>Both are non-experimental methods used to examine relationships between variables without manipulating them.</li><li>Both can produce quantitative data and use statistical analysis to interpret results.</li><li>Both can be conducted in naturalistic settings.</li></ul>For more information on correlational studies, see Chapter 1.	<ul><li>A survey is a method of gathering data, while a **correlational study** is a research design that tests the relationship between two or more variables.</li><li>Surveys can collect a broad range of data, including attitudes, opinions and behaviours, while correlational studies focus specifically on measuring how strongly variables are related.</li><li>Surveys may include open-ended and closed-ended questions, whereas correlational studies require numerical data to calculate **correlation coefficients**.</li></ul>

Table 2.2: The similarities and differences between surveys and other research methods

2.2 Analysing survey and questionnaire data

All of you will study data analysis and interpretation, to learn core analysis skills. However, **only HL students** will be assessed on it.

In this chapter, you will look at quantitative data analysis. For qualitative data analysis, refer to Chapter 4 to find information on **thematic analysis**.

Researchers using quantitative methods apply two types of statistical analysis:

- **Descriptive statistics** summarise the data but do not indicate causation.
- **Inferential statistics** measure the probability that the relationship between variables is due to chance, in order to determine causality. For more on inferential statistics, refer to Chapter 3.

Use the decision tree in **Figure 2.1** to help you decide which type of statistical analysis to use on your survey data.

1. What type of data does your survey collect?

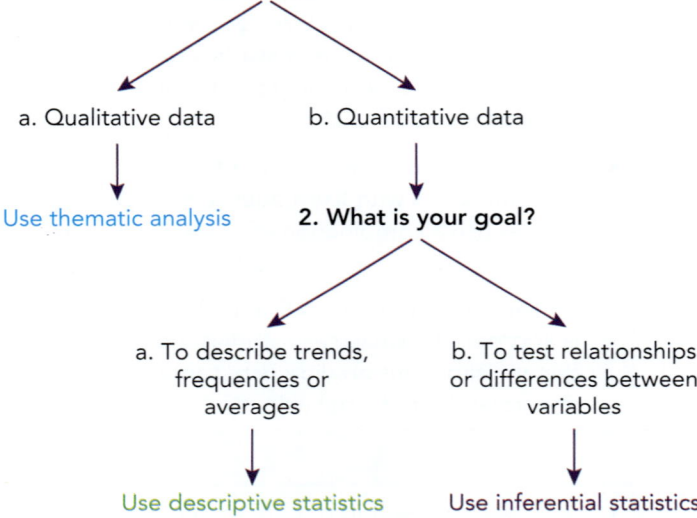

a. Qualitative data   b. Quantitative data

Use thematic analysis   **2. What is your goal?**

a. To describe trends, frequencies or averages

b. To test relationships or differences between variables

Use descriptive statistics   Use inferential statistics

Figure 2.1: Deciding which type of statistical analysis to conduct.

Types of data

Before you begin analysing your data, it is important to know the type of data you have collected (**Table 2.3**).

Type of data	Description	For example...	Measure of central tendency
Nominal data	Categorical data, used with named categories in which there is no ranking in the data	Colours. It is not possible to rank one colour higher than another.	The **mode**, the most frequently occurring value, is used with nominal data.
Ordinal data	Categorical data in which there is an order, and the data can be ranked	Bronze, silver and gold medals at a competition	The **median** can be used to identify the middle value in an ordered data set, which is often used when **outliers** are found in the data.

Type of data	Description	For example...	Measure of central tendency
Interval data	A type of numerical data that represents measured quantities; however, there is an arbitrary zero Continuous data, meaning the numerical data can take any value within a range	Temperature in degrees Celsius	The **mean**, the total of all values which is divided by the number of values, is used with interval data, provided there are no outliers.
Ratio data	A type of numerical data that has a true zero, allowing multiplication Continuous data	Grams, where you can say 100 grams is half of 200 grams.	Both the mean and median can be used. If there are outliers, the median should be used.

Table 2.3: Different data types, examples and common measures of central tendency

Data analysis: Descriptive statistics

Step 1: Assess the distribution and outliers

A key first step in analysing survey data is to examine the distribution of responses, which refers to how the values in a data set are spread across the range of possible scores. This helps psychologists determine whether the data follows a **normal distribution** (a symmetrical, bell-shaped curve) or is **skewed**, meaning the scores cluster more to one side.

In a normal distribution (**Figure 2.2a**), the mean, median and mode are roughly equal, and the **standard deviation (SD)** accurately reflects how spread out the scores are from the mean (see Step 2). However, in a skewed distribution (**Figure 2.2b**), the mean is pulled toward the tail, which can misrepresent the 'typical' score. In such cases, the median may be a more accurate **measure of central tendency**, and the SD may not fully capture the variability in the data. Recognising whether data is normal or skewed is essential for choosing the right statistical analyses and accurately interpreting results.

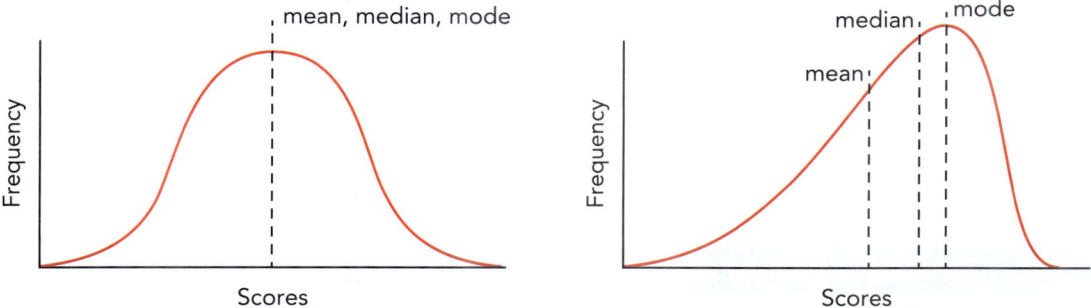

Figure 2.2: a Normal distribution; b Skewed distribution

After assessing the distribution, you need to identify any outliers. These are extreme scores that fall far outside the main pattern of responses. Outliers can distort your data analysis, so it is important to check for them before choosing your descriptive statistics.

For example, if most participants rate physical attraction as 5 or 6 out of 7, but one person rates it as 1, that score may be an outlier.

A common method for identifying outliers uses the **interquartile range (IQR)**:

- **Lower threshold** = Q1 − (1.5 × IQR)
- **Upper threshold** = Q3 + (1.5 × IQR)

You can consider any value below or above these thresholds an outlier. However, outliers are sometimes left in the data set if the sample size is low, which then affects the inferential statistics. This is discussed in Chapter 3.

Outliers are important because they can inflate the mean and SD, making the data appear more variable than they really are. In such cases, using the median and the IQR (instead of the mean and SD) can give a more accurate summary of the data.

Step 2: Calculate measures of central tendency and dispersion

Measures of central tendency are used to find the centre of the data set. These include:

- **Mean**: The average. Add up all the scores and divide by how many there are. The mean works best with normally distributed data.
- **Median**: The middle score. Arrange all the scores in numerical order to find the middle one. The median is less affected by outliers or skewed data, making it a useful alternative to the mean.
- **Mode**: The most frequently occurring score in the data set.

Measures of dispersion show how much variability there is in a set of responses, which helps psychologists to see how consistent the participants' answers were. High variability suggests large individual differences; low variability indicates consistency in responses. The most common measures of dispersion are:

- **Standard deviation (SD)**: This is a measure of how spread out the scores are around the mean in a set of data. If the SD is low, the scores are close to the mean, meaning that the participants had similar responses. If the SD is high, the scores are more spread out and there is more variation in the responses.
- **Interquartile range (IQR)**: This describes the spread of the middle 50 per cent of scores (from Q1 to Q3). It is helpful when data includes outliers, as it is less influenced by extreme values than the SD.
- **Variation ratio (VR)**: This shows the proportion of responses that are **not** in the mode category. It is used for nominal data to indicate how concentrated responses are around a single category.

Table 2.4 provides a summary of the measures of central tendency and dispersion to use with different types of data.

Data type	Measure of central tendency	Measure of dispersion
Nominal	Mode	VR
Ordinal	Median or mode	IQR
Interval	Mean (if normal), median (if skewed)	SD (if normal), IQR (if skewed)
Ratio	Mean (if normal), median (if skewed)	SD (if normal), IQR (if skewed)

Table 2.4: Data types and their measures of central tendency and dispersion

Activity 1: Data handling

A student surveyed 12 participants (aged 18–24 years) on which factors they found most attractive when dating. Each participant rated four factors on a Likert scale.

Table 2.5 shows the student's results.

Participant	Appearance	Shared interests	Shared values	Location
Participant 1	4	3	5	5
Participant 2	5	3	4	4
Participant 3	3	4	5	3
Participant 4	2	5	4	4
Participant 5	5	4	5	5
Participant 6	4	4	3	4
Participant 7	4	3	4	1
Participant 8	5	4	5	4
Participant 9	3	3	3	3
Participant 10	2	4	4	3
Participant 11	3	5	5	4
Participant 12	5	4	4	5

Table 2.5: Data collected from attraction survey

Using the raw data in **Table 2.5**, answer the questions.

1. Calculate the mean, median, mode and standard deviation for each factor.

2. Which factor has the lowest standard deviation? What does this suggest about the consistency of responses?

3. Use the interquartile range (IQR) method to calculate the lower and upper outlier thresholds for each factor. Identify any responses that fall outside these thresholds.

    The calculation is:

    *   Lower threshold = Q1 − (1.5 × IQR)
    *   Upper threshold = Q3 + (1.5 × IQR)

Step 3: Visualise the data

You will create a **graph** to visualise your data. In doing so, it is important to ensure you label the graph axes correctly and include a brief explanation indicating what the graph shows.

Table 2.6 provides an overview of which graph you should use for each data type.

Data type	Graph type
Nominal (categories, no order)	Bar graph
Ordinal (ordered categories)	Bar graph
Interval ratio (continuous, numerical data)	Histogram, line graph, scatterplot, box and whisker plot, frequency table

Table 2.6: Graph types for each data type

Graphing techniques

Frequency table

What it shows: A **frequency table** shows how often each value or category occurs. It lists all possible responses or scores in one column and the number of times (frequency) each occurs in another (**Table 2.7**). This may be cumulative frequency (a running total of frequencies) or relative frequency (percentage of the total).

Category	Frequency
Category A	15
Category B	5
Category C	4
Category D	6
Category E	1

Table 2.7: An example of a frequency table

When to use it: When you have raw data and want to analyse it as a first step before creating a graph.

Common errors:

- Not labelling columns correctly
- Unequal or overlapping intervals, which can distort the data
- Not checking that the totals are correct

Activity 2: Drawing conclusions

Table 2.8 shows how teachers rated the importance of building positive relationships in the classroom (with 1 being not important at all and 5 being very important).

What conclusions can you draw from **Table 2.8**?

Importance in the classroom	Frequency (number of teachers)
1	3
2	10
3	16
4	12
5	24

Table 2.8: Frequency table rating the importance of building positive relationships in the classroom

Bar graph

What it shows: In a **bar graph**, each bar represents a category and the height shows how many participants fall into that category (**Figure 2.3**). The height of each bar represents the value of each category, and is useful for comparing values quickly.

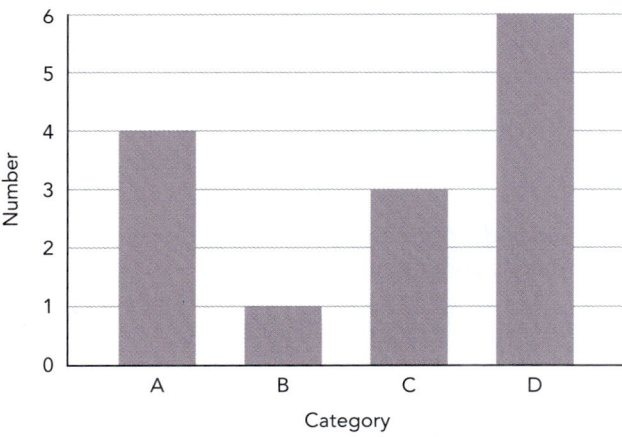

Figure 2.3: An example of a bar graph

When to use it: A bar graph is one of the most common ways in which to display categorical data or discrete data using rectangular bars.

Common errors:

- Using a bar graph for continuous data (use a histogram)
- Drawing the bars so they touch, which incorrectly suggests continuity
- Incorrectly labelling the axes or omitting the labels
- Distorting the y-axis (for example not starting at zero), which can exaggerate the visual differences
- Including too many categories, reducing its readability

Histogram

What it shows: A **histogram** is a type of graph that shows the distribution of continuous data (**Figure 2.4**). It displays how frequently values occur within equal-sized intervals, or bins, along a number line on the x-axis. The y-axis shows the frequency.

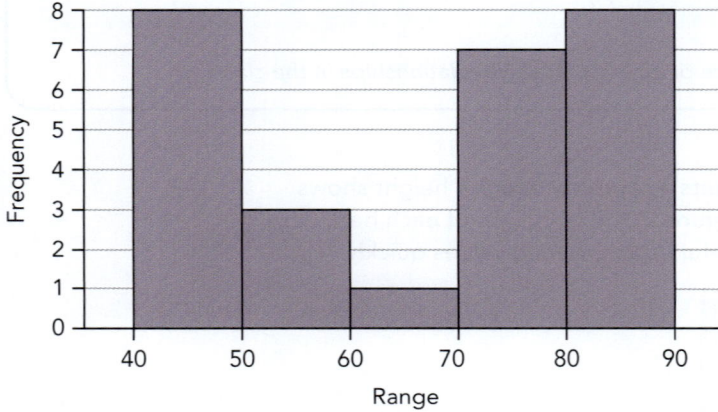

Figure 2.4: An example histogram

When to use it: A histogram is mainly used to show the frequency distribution of continuous data. The bars touch each other to show that the data is continuous.

Common errors:

- Using a histogram for categorical data (use a bar chart)
- Unequal bin widths, which can be misleading during interpretation
- Frequency labels on the y-axis may be missing
- Too many or too few bins, which can obscure patterns

Box and whiskers plot

What it shows: A **box and whisker plot**, or box plot, is especially useful when you are trying to understand how your data is spread out and whether any values stand out as unusual. Imagine you have test scores from a class. Rather than looking at all the numbers individually, a box plot summarises them using five key markers: the smallest score, the lower quartile (the bottom 25 per cent of scores), the median (the middle score), the upper quartile (the top 25 per cent of scores) and the highest score. These five values comprise the 'box' and two 'whiskers' (**Figure 2.5**).

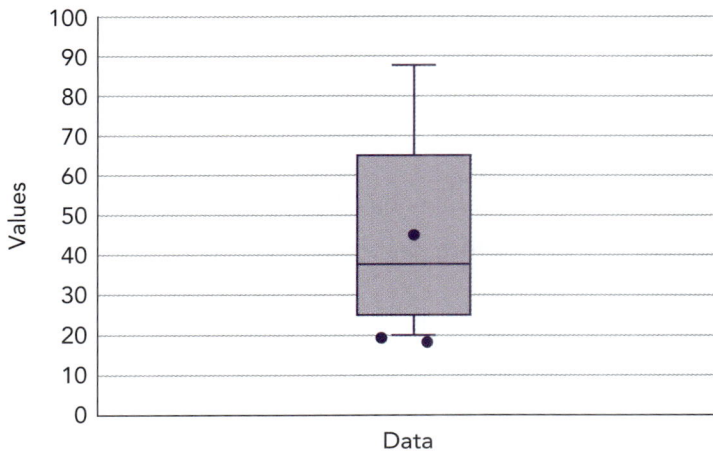

Figure 2.5: *An example box and whisker plot*

When to use it: Box plots are useful in visualising outliers, which will often be shown as individual points beyond the whiskers. This makes box plots ideal when comparing multiple sets of data, because you can quickly see which group has a higher median, or more spread.

Common errors:

- Misinterpreting the box width as indicating the number of (it shows data spread)
- Using box plots for very small samples. In this instance, quartiles become unreliable
- Failing to report or explain outliers shown beyond the whiskers

Line graph

What it shows: A **line graph** connects data points in the order they occur, from left to right, which makes it easy to identify trends in your data (**Figure 2.6**).

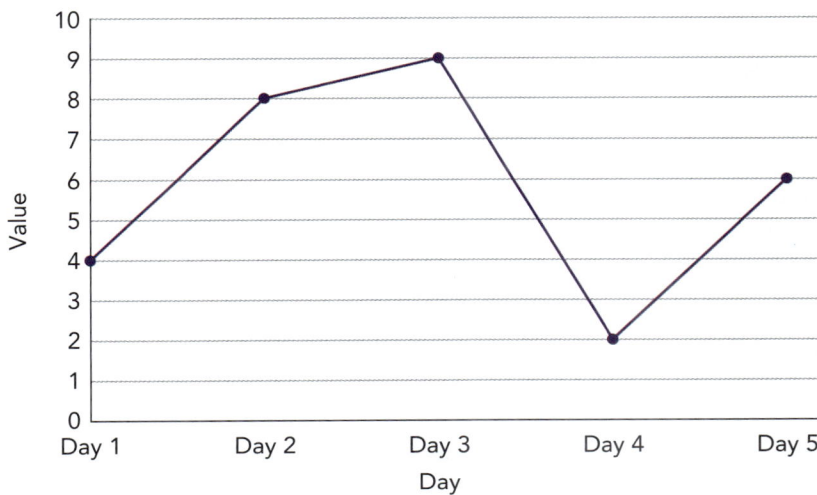

Figure 2.6: *An example line graph*

When to use it: A line graph is useful to track changes over time. For example, if you want to see how relationship satisfaction changed over a month, a line graph can help you spot the peaks and lows. The x-axis usually shows time, with the y-axis showing the factor being measured.

Common errors:

- Using a line graph for categorical data; line graphs are meant for continuous data
- Missing or uneven intervals on the x-axis, and uneven spacing distorts the trend and misleads the viewer
- Not connecting the points in a logical order (connect points sequentially)
- Plotting individual data points instead of means, which affects the clarity and readability of the graph

Scatterplot

What it shows: A **scatterplot** shows the relationship between two continuous variables by plotting individual data points. A **line of best fit** indicates the strength and direction of the relationship (**Figure 2.7**).

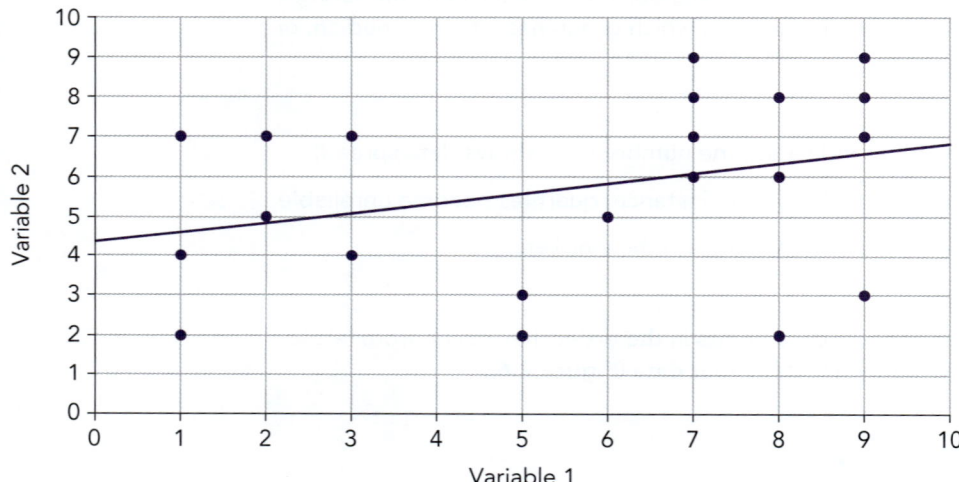

Figure 2.7: An example scatterplot

When to use it: You can use a scatterplot to explore the relationship between two continuous variables. This graph is useful for:

- indicating the strength and direction of a correlation, whether positive (both variables increase at the same time) or negative (as one variable increases, the other decreases)
- identifying where there is no correlation or there are outliers in the data.

Common errors:

- Assuming correlation means causation (scatterplots only show association)
- Not describing the type or strength of the relationship
- Ignoring outliers, for example a single extreme point may make a weak relationship appear stronger (or vice versa)
- Plotting means or summary data instead of individual data points (scatterplot should show individual cases, not averages)

Activity 3: Which graph should you use?

For each of the following research questions, identify the most appropriate graphing technique. Remember, this depends on the type of data collected.

1. Does argument frequency increase six months into a relationship?
2. Is there a relationship between stress and the number of arguments?
3. How does argument frequency vary by age group?
4. Are financial struggles or communication a bigger source of conflict in couples?
5. How long do arguments usually last between married couples?

HL Correlation coefficient

For Paper 3, you will need to show that you know how to analyse correlational research. The key aim of a correlation study is to investigate the relationship between two continuous variables. For example, is there a correlation between good communication skills and the duration of marriages? Correlational studies are used when it may not be ethical or practical to manipulate a variable, allowing an exploration of a relationship to inform future research.

The closer the data points are to the line of best fit on a scatterplot, the stronger the correlation. Following this, a statistical test can be undertaken to identify the correlation coefficient.

The **Pearson's r test** can be used to determine both the strength and direction of the relationship, but only when the data is normally distributed. The + or − indicates whether the relationship is positive or negative. The closer the value of r is to +1 or −1, the stronger the relationship between the variables. Values near 0 suggest that there is no relationship between the two variables.

Key Concept: Causality

Correlations allow researchers to see whether two variables are related, and how strongly. However, sometimes an additional factor can give a misleading relationship, known as a spurious variable. To determine cause and effect, researchers need to use experimental methods that involve manipulating variables and controlling variables.

Reflection activity

A psychologist examined daily social media use and the breakdown of communication in relationships, with 200 participants completing a survey. It asked about social media use frequency and had a 5-point Likert scale assessing how often they had conflict (1 = never and 5 = always). The Pearson r test found $r = +0.62$.

1. What does the correlation coefficient indicate about social media use and the breakdown of communication in relationships?
2. Are there any third variables that could influence this result?

2.3 Class practical planning worksheet
Surveys

This worksheet will help you prepare for Paper 2 Section A Question 1. A blank version can be downloaded from collins.co.uk/internationalresources. Ensure that you design and record your class practical clearly enough for it to be used as the basis for the exam. You can record your answers in a copy of the *Class practical recording sheet* (refer to Chapter 1). An idea for your class practical could be to explore how communication changes based on context – *school vs home, online vs offline*.

Aim and research question

What is the title and aim of your investigation?	
What is your research question?	
What is the specific area of human relationships you are exploring? Have you conducted background research on this issue?	*Consider the specific aspect of human relationships that you are investigating, and existing research that you may be able to draw on.*
Why is this worth exploring in your school or community context?	

Sampling technique and size

What sampling method will you use (for example, random, stratified, opportunity), and why?	
Will you use an online platform to gather your data?	
How many participants will you include?	*You must collect data from at least 10 participants. Consider how you will do this efficiently.*

Procedure

Will your survey questions produce quantitative data (for example numbers on a scale) or qualitative data (for example written responses)?	*Think about how this will affect your analysis. Quantitative data allows statistical analysis, and qualitative data will be analysed thematically.*
What is the estimated completion time? Will you use open- or closed-ended questions, or both?	
Are you using an existing scale or measurement tool?	
What steps will you take to protect participants' rights and conduct ethical research?	*You should consider confidentiality, informed consent, the right to withdraw and debriefing.*

Data collection

Have you pilot tested your questions to check for clarity?	
How will you phrase questions to avoid bias or leading questions?	
What format will the survey be in (for example, online, face to face)?	
Which key concepts are relevant in your practical, and why?	

Data analysis

Which measure of central tendency and dispersion will you use?	
Which graphing technique will be most appropriate, and why?	
What errors do you need to be aware of when analysing your results?	

Discussion

What are the main threats to validity or reliability?	
How could bias be present in your research?	*Consider how to minimise bias, for example sampling bias or social desirability.*
How could your findings be useful? Consider both short-term and long-term applications.	

2.4 Apply it! Paper 2 practice questions

1a. Describe how a survey or questionnaire was used in your class practical.   **(4 marks)**

Sample answer	Notes
We used a survey method in our class practical to identify perceived barriers to student-teacher communication. Our aim was to explore the extent to which students felt comfortable approaching teachers, and what factors influenced this.	Topic and aim are clearly indicated at the start.
We used a volunteer sample of Year 12 students. At the end of an assembly, we displayed a poster with a QR code for the online survey. This also included a brief explanation of the study, our contact details and an informed consent form.	
The survey comprised six different statements using a Likert scale, where 1 = never to 4 = very often. For example, 'I feel too busy to ask my teacher questions.' These were followed by two open-ended questions, including: 'What would make communication easier?.'	Demonstrates understanding of the research method, and links to how this was used in the class practical.
We piloted the questions beforehand to ensure clarity and appropriate length. We informed participants that they did not need to answer every question and could withdraw at any time, and that their responses would remain anonymous. Nineteen students completed the survey.	Accurate use of psychological terminology throughout.

1b. Explain bias in relation to your class practical.   **(4 marks)**

Sample answer	Notes
Bias refers to errors in the sampling, design or measurement of a study, which could reduce the validity or generalisability of the findings.	Clear definition of the concept.
Firstly, there could have been sampling bias, as we used volunteer sampling. This introduces self-selection bias, in which those with stronger views on teacher communication may have been more likely to respond, making them unrepresentative of the wider Year 12 cohort. It also may not have represented students who rarely communicate with teachers, as taking part in a survey on teacher-student relationships might itself feel like a form of school engagement. Sampling bias may have reduced the population validity of our study. One way to reduce sampling bias would have been to use stratified sampling instead of volunteer sampling to broaden our sample.	Two types of bias are explained and linked explicitly to the class practical.
Another type of bias is social desirability bias, in which participants may answer in a way that presents them more positively. In the case of our topic (student-teacher relationships), some students may have been reluctant to express negative views, even though responses were anonymous. This could have led to an underreporting of any barriers to communication, affecting the validity of the results.	

Now you try it

Practise these Paper 2 Section A questions based on your survey/questionnaire class practical. You could try them in timed conditions, in which case, only give yourself 20 minutes. Remember to ask your teacher for feedback!

1a. Describe how a survey or questionnaire was used in your class practical. **(4 marks)**

1b. Explain responsibility in relation to your class practical. **(4 marks)**

HL 2.5 Apply it! HL focus

Paper 3 Question 1 requires you to explain one issue that limits the interpretation of the information presented in Source 1 (this will be provided with the question).

In this section, you will see an example of a strong response to this question. Then, you will have the opportunity to practise writing your own answer using the same source.

The example sources in the Apply it! sections in Chapters 2–5 have been collated to assess the claim that screen time before going to sleep can negatively affect adolescents' academic performance.

Source 1 shows the effect sleep has on student academic performance.

Source 1

The link between sleep and student academic performance

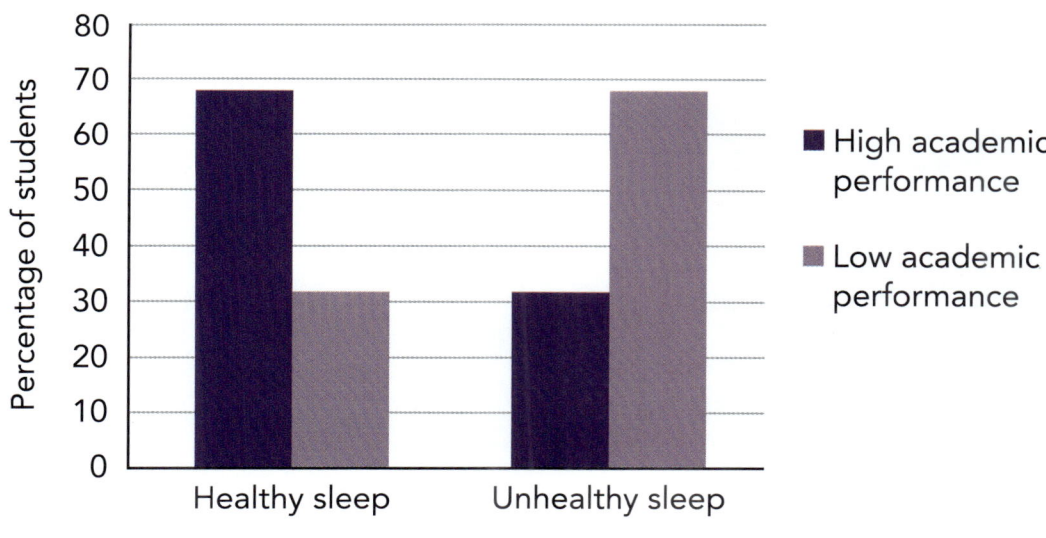

1. Explain **one** issue that limits the interpretation of the data in **Source 1**. **(3 marks)**

Sample answer	Notes
One issue that may limit the interpretation of the data in Source 1 is that the bars in the graph are touching, a convention reserved for continuous data (in histograms). However, the variables in this graph are categorical and discrete (sleep and level of academic performance). Presenting them as continuous may lead to the misinterpretation of a progression between groups that does not exist, and mislead people into believing that there is a statistical relationship between sleep habits and academic performance that is not valid.	The first sentence identifies what the issue is, the second explains why this is and issue, and then the final sentence explains how this limits interpretation. Try using this structure: 1. What? 2. Why? 3. So What?

Now you try it

Using the same **Source 1**, identify *another* issue that could be explained.

1. Explain **one** issue that limits the interpretation of the data in **Source 1**.

(3 marks)

Learning and cognition: Experiments

For the context Learning and cognition, you need to be able to plan and conduct an **experiment**. Experiments are effective because they allow researchers to test mental processes, such as memory, under controlled conditions to gather **quantitative** data.

You can apply the key concepts in **Table 3.1** to experiments.

Concept	Application
Bias	**Demand characteristics** can threaten **internal validity**, where participants guess the study's aim. Use a **single-blind design** or a **double-blind design**, filler tasks and standardised instructions to limit this bias.
Causality	You can use experiments to establish cause-and-effect relationships by manipulating the **independent variable** and controlling **extraneous variables**, while measuring the **dependent variable**.
Change	Use pre- and post-tests, or between-group comparisons, to quantify the effect of the independent variable on the dependent variable. You can then use effect-size statistics to quantify the significance of the observed change (refer to section 3.4).
Measurement	The measurement of an experiment depends on clear **operationalisation** – for example, clearly defining the variables and stating how you will measure them. Validating and using reliable measures will ensure accurate results. Using pilot tests and inter-rater checks will strengthen **construct validity** and **reliability**.
Perspective	Experiments reflect **reductionist** and **positivist** views, focusing on isolating variables.
Responsibility	Researchers must secure informed consent, justify any deception, minimise harm and provide a full debrief, in line with ethical guidelines.

Table 3.1: The six key concepts and their application to experiments

3.1 Introduction to experiments

What is an experiment?

Psychologists use experiments to study the causes of human behaviour. They are a way of testing a hypothesis. In an experiment, you manipulate the independent variable (IV) and measure effect on the dependent variable (DV), while controlling any extraneous variables. For example, in Bandura's (1961) study into social learning (refer to Chapter 1), the IV was exposure to aggressive or non-aggressive adult behaviour, and the DV was the amount of aggressive behaviour shown by the child in the test situation.

In your class practical, you must choose to conduct either a **true experiment** or a **quasi-experiment** with a **minimum of five participants** (refer to Table 3.3). It must be conducted during lesson time unless a teacher-signed class-practical research form is completed.

Planning an experiment

When planning your experiment, use the following sequence to ensure your study is valid, reliable and ethically sound.

Step 1: Operationalise the variables

First, identify the independent and dependent variables, and then explain how you will operationalise – manipulate and measure – them. You must operationalise the IV in a way that reflects a meaningful and controlled manipulation, and measure the DV in a way that accurately captures the effect of that manipulation. Effective operationalisation enhances construct validity, ensuring the study truly measures what it intends to. Without this, the **validity** of the conclusions may be compromised.

For example, imagine conducting a study to whether listening to Mozart improves memory. You would need to be able to precisely operationalise both the IV and the DV:

- **IV (listening to Mozart):** Participants are either exposed to 10 minutes of Mozart or sit in silence while studying.

- **DV (memory performance):** The number of words correctly recalled from a list of 20 nouns.

By clearly defining the IV and DV, the experiment can be replicated and any observed effects can be confidently attributed to the manipulation of the IV.

Step 2: Write the hypothesis

You then formulate a hypothesis. This is a testable prediction about how the IV will affect the DV.

- The **null hypothesis (H_0)** states that there will be *no effect* of the IV on the DV. Researchers aim to reject the null hypothesis to demonstrate a possible link between the IV and DV. If a result is significant, we reject the null hypothesis. This is established during the analysis, known as statistical testing (refer to section 3.4). For example: *There will be no significant difference in the number of words recalled between students who study with background Mozart music and those who study in silence.*

- The **research (or alternative) hypothesis (H_1)** predicts the effect of the IV on the DV. There are two types of research or alternative hypotheses:

  o Directional, or one-tailed, indicating the direction of the relationship. For example: *Participants in condition B (Mozart) will recall significantly more words than those in condition A (silence).*

  o Non-directional, or two-tailed, indicating that there is a relationship but not in which direction. For example: *There will be a difference in the number of words recalled depending on whether the participants listen to Mozart or study in silence.*

> ### Key concept: Causality
>
> True experiments offer high control and random assignment, which enhances internal validity and the precision of measurement when assessing cause-and-effect relationships. However, this control can reduce external validity, as the artificial setting may not reflect real-world behaviour. In contrast, quasi-experiments have less control and no random assignment, which may weaken internal validity and measurement precision but improve generalisability.

Step 3: Control extraneous variables

To ensure the results are valid, researchers aim to control extraneous variables. These are any variables other than the IV that could affect the DV. Common controls include keeping the same environment, time of day, materials or instructions for all participants. For example, in the memory performance study, use the same word list and piece of Mozart's music, and keep the setting and timings the same.

Uncontrolled variables may become **confounding variables**, which threaten the internal validity of the study.

Step 4: Decide on the experimental design

Once you have written your hypothesis, the next step is to choose an **experimental design**. This is how participants will be assigned to the different conditions of your experiment (**Table 3.2**). Each design has its own strengths and limitations. The best choice depends on the nature of the study and the variables involved.

Design	Definition	For example...	Strengths	Limitations
Independent measures	Participants are randomly assigned to one condition, meaning they only take part in one level of the IV.	They are either in condition A (silence) or condition B (Mozart).	• No order effects • Less chance of guessing the aim	• **Participant variability** differences between individuals (for example, memory ability, motivation, prior knowledge) can affect the results. • More participants are required.
Repeated measures	Each participant completes all conditions of the experiment.	Each participant performs condition A (silence) and condition B (Mozart).	• Controls participant variables • Fewer participants needed	**Order effects** (order of the conditions) may affect the result: • **Practice effect** (performance improves due to repetition). • **Fatigue effect** (performance worsens due to tiredness, boredom, loss of concentration). Have participants complete the conditions in different orders (**counterbalancing**) to reduce this bias.

Design	Definition	For example...	Strengths	Limitations
Matched pairs	Pair individuals based on a relevant characteristic before assigning each person in the pair to a different condition.	Participants can be matched based on their cognitive ability or age, for example.	• Controls for participant variables without order effects • Groups are more equivalent at the start	• Time-consuming matching participants. • Data loss if a participant drops out.

Table 3.2: Different experimental designs

Using the right design improves internal validity and helps ensure that differences in the DV can be confidently attributed to the IV, rather than participant characteristics or the structure of the task itself.

Step 5: Choose the type of experiment

In psychology, there are several types of experiments, each with different levels of control and real-world applicability. For your class practical, you will choose either a true experiment or a quasi-experiment (**Table 3.3**).

Experiment	True experiment (section 3.2)	Quasi-experiment (section 3.3)
Definition	True experiments take place in a controlled environment, such as a lab. The researcher manipulates the IV. Participants are randomly assigned to conditions, which allows researchers to establish cause-and-effect relationships.	Quasi-experiments also take place in a controlled environment, such as a lab, and the researcher manipulates the IV. However, groups are based on pre-existing characteristics (for example, year group). This limits causal inference because groups are not randomly assigned.
Use	When the researcher can randomly assign participants to conditions and manipulate the IV in a controlled setting.	When random allocation is not practical or ethical and the goal is to compare groups based on an existing characteristic.
Limitations	• No random assignment, which can lower internal validity. • Pre-existing groups may share characteristics, which can limit population validity. • Higher risk of confounding variables influencing results.	• The artificial setting can reduce the **ecological validity.** • Ethical or practical constraints may limit manipulation. • Demand characteristics may influence participant behaviour.

Table 3.3: The different types of experiment that you can use in your class practical

Activity 1: Practising planning an experiment

Imagine your school is reviewing its digital device policy. Some teachers at the school argue that students should take notes by hand to better retain information, while others say typing is more efficient and just as effective for learning.

As a student psychologist, the head of your school has asked you to design an experiment to test whether writing by hand really does improve memory more than typing. Complete the following tasks.

1. Operationalise the IV and DV.
2. State the null and research hypotheses.
3. Identify the variables you would need to control.
4. Decide on the most suitable experimental design for this study.
5. Decide which type of experiment you will use, and justify your choice.

Compare and contrast It!: Paper 2 Question 1c

Experiments versus other research methods

Paper 2 Section A Question **1c** will ask you to compare and contrast your experiment with another research method. You have already compared the use of experiments with surveys (section 2.1). Use **Table 3.4** to help plan your response for other research methods.

Remember that in the exam you will need to discuss each similarity and difference in detail. For example:

Experiments aim to establish causal relationships by manipulating variables under controlled conditions, allowing researchers to isolate effects and draw generalisable conclusions. In contrast, case studies focus on the detailed exploration of a single individual or small group, often in real-life contexts, without the manipulation of variables. While experiments prioritise control and replicability, case studies emphasise depth, context and the complexity of psychological experience.

Similarities	Differences
Experiments vs interviews	
<ul><li>Both follow a planned and consistent method of collecting data.</li><li>Both can explore relationships between variables, allowing researchers to identify patterns or associations.</li><li>Experimental methods share procedural consistency with structured and semi-structured interviews, to ensure standardisation across participants.</li></ul> For more information on interviews, see Chapter 4.	<ul><li>Experiments are designed to establish causal links by manipulating variables, whereas interviews explore participants' perspectives and lived experiences without testing causality.</li><li>Experiments focus on generalising findings through hypothesis testing, while interviews aim for depth of understanding within a particular context or population.</li><li>Experiments are highly standardised to maintain control and internal validity, while interviews allow for flexibility and follow-up.</li></ul>

Similarities	Differences
Experiments vs observations	
• Both can involve systematic data collection to ensure reliability and consistency. • Both can be conducted in controlled lab environments or more naturalistic field settings. • Both may include quantitative data, such as frequencies or duration of behaviours. For more information on observations, see Chapter 5.	• Experiments involve the manipulation of an IV and control over extraneous factors. Observations do not involve manipulation and offer limited control over the environment. • Experiments aim to show causality, whereas observations identify patterns and associations but cannot determine cause-and-effect relationships. • Experiments often occur in artificial settings with lower ecological validity. Observations are usually conducted in real-world environments, thereby increasing ecological validity.
Experiments vs case studies	
• Both can gather quantitative data. • Both can be conducted in naturalistic settings. • Both look at relationships. However, experiments focus on causality. For more information on case studies, see Chapter 1.	• Experiments involve the manipulation of variables and control over conditions, while case studies are observational and typically lack control. • Experiments typically use larger, structured samples, while case studies often focus on a single individual or small group. • Experiments aim for generalisable results, whereas case studies provide in-depth, context-rich data, but are less generalisable.
Experiments vs correlational studies	
• Both examine relationships between variables. • Both can use quantitative data and apply statistical analysis. • Both can inform theory development and can predict behaviour. For more information on correlational studies, see Chapter 1.	• Experiments test cause-and-effect, whereas correlational studies identify associations without proving causation. • Experiments involve manipulating the IV, but correlational studies involve no manipulation, just measurement of existing variables. • Experiments require controlled conditions, and correlational studies often take place in the natural environment.

Table 3.4: The similarities and differences between experiments and other research methods

Study in focus

Tversky and Kahneman (1974): Anchoring bias and questions

Researchers have found that people tend to rely heavily on the first piece of information they hear (the anchor) when making decisions, even if it's irrelevant or arbitrary. This can lead to anchoring bias, and this effect was studied by Tversky and Kahneman (1974), who conducted an experiment to investigate whether anchoring affects judgements.

Two groups of high school students estimated, within five seconds, a numerical question that was written on the blackboard. One group estimated the product of $8 \times 7 \times 6 \times 5 \times 4 \times 3 \times 2 \times 1$ while another group estimated the product of $1 \times 2 \times 3 \times 4 \times 5 \times 6 \times 7 \times 8$. The actual answer is 40 320. Controls were taken in the experiment, such as standardising the time to five seconds to make the estimation.

It was found that the group with the low anchor, which had an ascending sequence starting with 1, estimated lower than the high anchor condition with the descending sequence starting with 8. They concluded that anchors can inform subsequent decisions.

Reflection

1. What were the independent and dependent variables in this study?

2. Which research design was used?

Tversky, A. and Kahneman, D. (1974). Judgment under uncertainty: Heuristics and biases. *Science, 185*, 1124–1131.

Responsibility

Being an ethical researcher

When studying learning and cognition, researchers have a responsibility to ensure participants are protected, respected and supported throughout the study. In line with IB ethical guidelines, you need to adhere to the following points in your class practical.

- **Informed consent**: You need to have parental consent for any participants under the age of 16 years.

- **Deception**: Sometimes, researchers may withhold the true purpose of a study on learning and cognition in order to avoid demand characteristics. Participants can be deliberately given false information (commission), or information about the true aim of the study can be withheld (omission). You can only use partial deception for your class practical if it is harmless and your participants are fully debriefed. Your teacher needs to approve your class practical.

- **Right to withdraw**: When providing consent to participate, ensure participants know that they can leave the experiment at any time, especially if they feel anxious, frustrated or mentally exhausted during complex cognitive tasks.

- **Data protection**: It is important that you keep any scores on cognitive tasks confidential and do not share them beyond your class practical. You must anonymise the data and delete the files after use.

- **Restrictions**: You are not permitted to use animals in your class practical. You also cannot conduct experiments involving obedience and conformity.

3.2 True experiments

The term 'true experiment' is used to distinguish this method from other experimental designs, as it meets specific scientific criteria required to establish a causal relationship. These criteria include:

- manipulation of an IV and measurement of a DV
- random allocation of participants to conditions
- control of extraneous variables
- hypothesis testing, including null and research hypotheses.

> **Key concept: Causality**
>
> One of the key strengths of true experiments is their high internal validity, achieved through the manipulation of the IV, control of extraneous variables and random assignment of participants. This allows for clear conclusions about cause-and-effect relationships.

True experiments often have high reliability due to the standardised procedures and controlled setting. However, due to the controlled nature of true experiments, they may not reflect real-world situations or the complexity of natural cognitive processes. Ecological validity refers to how well the findings of a study can be generalised to real-world settings. Often, the artificial tasks or settings do not resemble everyday life situations, which affects the **mundane realism**. For example, memorising a list of random words in a lab setting may not reflect how memory operates in natural contexts, such as studying for a test.

Participants are often aware that they are part of a study, which can lead to demand characteristics, which means they change their behaviour based on what they think the experiment is about. This may lead them to overperform, underperform or respond in a way they believe is expected. Researchers may use a single-blind design, in which participants are unaware of which condition they are in, or a double-blind design, in which neither the participant nor the researcher administering the experiment knows which condition the participant is in. This helps reduce demand characteristics and experimenter bias – the unintentional influence researchers may have on participants through their behaviour or expectations.

> **Study in focus**
>
> ## Loftus and Palmer (1974): Car crash experiment
>
> Loftus and Palmer (1974) investigated the effect of leading questions on memory.
>
> In their study, 45 participants watched seven driver education videos featuring car accidents. They then completed a survey with one critical question, such as, *'How fast were the cars going when they _____ each other?'* There were five conditions, each with a different verb in the question: contacted, hit, bumped, collided and smashed.
>
> Loftus and Palmer found that the verb influenced participants' speed estimates. Those who heard 'smashed' gave higher speed estimates than those who heard 'contacted'.
>
> This experiment showed how post-event information can distort memory recall, supporting the reconstructive nature of memory.
>
> ### Reflection
>
> 1. Name two controls taken in the study that increase the internal validity.
>
> 2. Why were participants shown driver education videos of a car accident?
>
> 3. How could the ecological validity be questioned in this study?
>
> Loftus, E. F. and Palmer, J. C. (1974). Reconstruction of automobile destruction: An example of the interaction between language and memory. *Journal of Verbal Learning and Verbal Behavior, 13*(5), 585–589.

3.3 Quasi-experiments

Researchers use quasi-experiments to examine the effects of the IV on the DV without randomly assigning participants to different conditions. Instead, they group participants based on pre-existing characteristics. Quasi-experiments are widely used in learning and cognition research because they allow psychologists to investigate how cognitive processes operate in real-world contexts or across naturally occurring non-equivalent groups, where random assignment is either unethical, impossible or impractical. For example, researchers might want to compare the working memory performance of students with and without attention deficit hyperactivity disorder (ADHD). In this case, participants cannot be randomly allocated. This method is particularly useful in cross-cultural research, as well as in **longitudinal** or **cross-sectional** designs, such as studying how cultural norms influence memory formation.

However, quasi-experiments are vulnerable to participant bias due to a lack of random assignment of participants. There could be pre-existing differences between the groups which can act as confounding variables (for example, motivation, prior experiences), making it difficult to determine whether the IV caused the observed effect. Quasi-experiments often have lower internal validity, and researchers must interpret their findings with caution.

> **Key concept: Bias**
>
> Researchers must avoid **publication bias** by ensuring that experimental data is reported regardless of the direction or statistical significance of the findings. Selectively publishing only positive or significant results distorts the findings, leading to a biased and incomplete understanding.

Study in focus

Maguire et al. (2000): London taxi drivers

Maguire et al. (2000) investigated whether extensive spatial navigation experience was associated with structural changes in the hippocampus. The hippocampus is a brain region associated with memory and learning, particularly spatial navigation. This study compared the brain structures of 16 right-handed male London taxi drivers, a group with extensive spatial navigation experience, to a control group of 50 right-handed male non-taxi drivers. By comparing participants with varying levels of navigation experience, the researchers were able to examine the direct effect of spatial experience on hippocampal structure. A number of controls were taken, such as taxi driver experience, and a range of ages were included. Magnetic Resonance Imaging (MRI) was used to measure both the size and density of the hippocampus.

The results showed that taxi drivers had significantly more grey matter volume in the posterior hippocampus, which is involved in storing and using spatial information. Non-taxi drivers showed more grey matter in the anterior hippocampus, which is associated with encoding new memories. Additionally, there was a positive correlation between the number of years spent driving taxis and the volume of the posterior hippocampus.

These findings support the theory that cognitive functions are localised in specific brain areas and demonstrate how prolonged spatial navigation demands may lead to structural changes in the hippocampus.

Reflection

1. Why was this study a quasi-experiment?

2. Why can a cause-and-effect relationship not be drawn?

Maguire, E. A., Gadian, D. G., Johnsrude, I. S., Good, C. D., Ashburner, J., Frackowiak, R. S. and Frith, C. D. (2000). Navigation-related structural change in the hippocampi of taxi drivers. *Proceedings of the National Academy of Sciences,* *97*(8), 4398–4403.

3.4 Analysing experimental data

All of you need to know how to analyse experimental data, to learn core analysis skills. However, **only HL students** will be assessed on data analysis and interpretation (in Paper 3).

In Chapter 2, you learned how to undertake **descriptive statistics**, which is the first step in your experimental analysis. Before calculating **inferential statistics** for your data, check that you have:

- **Calculated descriptive statistics**: Have you chosen the most representative **measure of central tendency** and **dispersion**? Have you checked for **outliers** in your data set?

- **Visualised your data**: Have you chosen the most appropriate way to represent your data based on the type of data collected?

Inferential statistics allow researchers to draw conclusions about a larger population based on data from a sample. Rather than simply describing data (as with descriptive statistics), inferential statistics are used to test hypotheses and assess whether the observed results are likely due to chance.

Statistical significance refers to the likelihood that an observed effect is not due to random variation. This is assessed using a *p*-value. A *p*-value represents the probability of obtaining the observed results, or a more extreme one, if the null hypothesis is true. It helps researchers decide whether any patterns in the data are meaningful or could have happened by random chance.

In psychology, the most commonly used significance level (α) is 0.05. This means the researcher accepts a 5 per cent probability of committing a **type I error** (rejecting a true null hypothesis). A small *p*-value (≤ 0.05) indicates that the outcome is unlikely under the null hypothesis and provides evidence to reject it. Conversely, a larger *p*-value (above 0.05) means there is not enough evidence to reject the null hypothesis, concluding that any observed pattern may be due to chance.

It is important to be able to identify the types of errors that can occur when interpreting *p*-values, as they help you understand the limitations of statistical conclusions and the risks of drawing incorrect inferences. **Table 3.5** distinguishes between the error types.

Error type	Explanation	How to reduce it
Type I error (false positive)	Rejecting the null hypothesis when it is actually true. You believe there is an effect, but in reality, there is none.	Use a lower confidence level (α = 0.01 instead of 0.05), which means you require stronger evidence in order to reject the null hypothesis.
Type II error (false negative)	Failing to reject the null hypothesis when it is actually false. You miss a real effect.	Use a larger sample size, which reduces random error and improves the ability to detect effects. Control extraneous variables to reduce variability in the data, making real effects easier to detect. Use accurate and reliable measurement tools to improve the sensitivity of your measurements and reduce measurement errors.

Table 3.5: Types of errors when interpreting the p-value

HL Choosing a statistical test

You are not required to choose a statistical test for your class practical write-up. However, if you are an HL student, you will find this section helpful for your Paper 3 assessment.

Selecting the right statistical test depends on three things:

1. The type of data you have:

   - **Nominal**: Categories with no order (for example, yes/no, eye colour (blue, brown, green).

Tip

There are several free online tools that you can use to perform statistical analysis, such as calculating *p*-values. Make sure you know whether your hypothesis is one-tailed (predicts a direction) or two-tailed (no predicted direction).

- **Ordinal**: Data with an order, but not evenly spaced (for example, a Likert scale from strongly agree to strongly disagree).

- **Interval/ratio**: Continuous numerical data with equal intervals between values. In IB Psychology, both are treated the same when choosing statistical tests. Interval data (for example, test scores, temperature) have meaningful differences between values but no true zero point. Ratio data (for example, reaction time, height, weight) also have equal intervals and include a true zero, allowing for meaningful ratios.

Refer to Chapter 2 for more information about the different data types.

2. Whether your data meets parametric assumptions (that is, it behaves normally). You can use a parametric test if all of these are true:

- Your DV is interval/ratio.

- Data is **normally distributed** (bell-shaped curve).

- Groups have homogeneous variance (a similar spread of data).

If your data does not meet these criteria, use a non-parametric test instead.

3. Your research design (for example, whether the same or different participants were used in each condition).

Table 3.6 provides a summary of the common statistical tests you can use.

Key concept: Perspective

Statistical significance testing has long been used in psychology to determine causality. However a fixed cut-off is often seen as arbitrary – a p-value of 0.049 is considered 'significant' while 0.051 is not, even though the difference is minimal. This can lead to overemphasis on numbers and underestimation of real-world meaning.

As psychology evolves as a science, there is a growing shift towards mixed-methods research, which combines statistical analysis with qualitative insights, providing a fuller understanding of human behaviour.

Data type	Research design	Parametric?	Statistical test
Nominal	Repeated measures (same participants)	–	Sign test
Nominal	Independent measures (different participants)	–	Chi-squared test
Ordinal or non-normal interval	Repeated measures	✗	Wilcoxon signed-rank test
Ordinal or non-normal interval	Independent measures	✗	Mann–Whitney U test
Normal interval/ratio	Repeated measures	✓	Paired samples t-test
Normal interval/ratio	Independent measures	✓	Independent samples t-test

Table 3.6: Common statistical tests

For Paper 3, it is important to understand how to interpret both descriptive and inferential statistics and draw valid conclusions.

Activity 2: Decisions about the null hypothesis

Scenario: A research study tested whether a small dose of caffeine (equivalent to half a cup of coffee) improved memory recall in students compared to a placebo. An independent measures design was used with eight participants in each group (caffeine vs placebo). After 10 minutes, the students in each condition completed a short memory task (maximum score 20). The result of the Mann-Whitney U test, using a significance level of 0.05, yielded a p-value of 0.08.

Table 3.7 presents descriptive statistics of caffeine and memory recall.

	Caffeine group	Placebo group
Mean	13.60	11.25
Standard deviation	1.06	1.03

Table 3.7: Some descriptive statistics for the study

1. Was the result statistically significant? What decision would you make about the null hypothesis?
2. How might the sample size have affected the outcome?

3.5 Class practical planning worksheet

Experiments

This worksheet will help you prepare for Paper 2 Section A Question 1. A blank version can be downloaded from collins.co.uk/internationalresources. Ensure that you design and record your class practical clearly enough to use as the basis for the exam. You can record your answers in a copy of the *Class practical recording sheet* (refer to Chapter 1). An idea for your class practical is to investigate the effect of leading questions on memory recall, replicating or adapting Loftus and Palmer's (1974) study. You could also plan a quasi-experiment to investigate whether participants from different cultural backgrounds differ in their vividness confidence or consistency of memory (flashbulb memory) for a significant public event (such as a major news story).

Aim and research question

What is the aim of your investigation?	
What is your null and research hypothesis?	
What is the specific issue or problem you are exploring? Have you conducted background research on the issue?	*Consider why it might be important to study the practical you have chosen, giving real-world contexts.*
Why is this worth exploring in your school or community context?	

Research methodology

How have you operationalised the IV and DV?	
What experimental design will you use? (For example, independent measures, repeated measures.) Why is this appropriate?	
If using a repeated measures design, outline your counterbalancing plan.	
What sampling method will you use? (For example, opportunity, random.) Why is it suitable for your experiment?	*If you are carrying out a true experiment, you will need to consider the age group that you will test.*
Who is your target population, and what sample size are you aiming for?	*You need a minimum of five participants per condition; large samples are beneficial for statistical tests.*
Which specific ethical considerations are you considering in the experiment? Will deception of the aim be used?	*If you intend to withhold the exact aim, you should consider how you will ensure that ethical standards are upheld. You should also ensure that you are minimising distress, and considering how you will debrief participants after the study.*

Data collection

How will you standardise your procedure to control for extraneous variables?	
What materials or stimuli will you use? (For example, video, word lists, timed tasks.)	*Ethical considerations are important in your choice of materials and stimuli.*
How will you record responses? (For example, a form, answer sheet.)	*Consider how you will ensure consistency in how you present the stimuli.*
Which key psychological concepts or theories are relevant to your experiment, and why?	

Data analysis

How will you calculate and report descriptive statistics?	*Consider mean, median and standard deviation.*
Which statistical test will you use, and why is it appropriate for your design and data type?	
How will you ensure your results are valid and your conclusions justified?	

Discussion

What are the main threats to validity or reliability?	
Could bias (for example, demand characteristics or researcher effects) affect your results? How will you control for this?	
How could your findings be applied in real-life settings? Consider both short-term applications (immediate use in schools) and long-term applications (policy changes).	

3.6 Apply it! Paper 2 practice questions

Section A Question **1c** asks you to compare the research method used in your class practical with an alternative method provided in the question. Look at the following example to see how this comparison can be effectively structured before attempting the response yourself.

1c. Compare and contrast the use of an experiment used in your class practical with an interview. **(6 marks)**

Sample answer	Notes
Both experiments and interviews use a structured and systematic approach to gather data. They often follow pre-defined procedures to ensure consistency and reliability. While experiments typically explore relationships through the manipulation of variables, interviews — especially structured or semi-structured — can also investigate associations by exploring themes or perceptions related to specific variables. Both methods can contribute valuable insights. However, interviews emphasise depth and context over quantifiable outcomes.	The first paragraph focuses on the similarities between the two methods.
Experiments are designed to test hypotheses and identify cause-and-effect relationships by manipulating an independent variable and measuring its effect on a dependent variable. They prioritise control, standardisation and internal validity. In contrast, interviews aim to explore personal experiences, beliefs or meanings in depth, making them more flexible and less controlled. Interviews do not test causality and are less focused on generalisation, instead, offering rich, contextualised data that reflects participants' unique perspectives	The second paragraph shows a direct contrast between the two methods.

Now you try it

1a. Describe how you used an experiment in your class practical, including the aim and procedure. **(4 marks)**

1b. Explain the concept of measurement in relation to your class practical. **(4 marks)**

1c. Compare and contrast the use of an experiment used in your class practical with an observation. **(6 marks)**

3.7 Apply it! HL focus

Paper 3 Question 2 requires you to analyse the findings from **Source 2** (provided in a separate Resource Booklet in the exam) and draw a clear, evidence-based conclusion.

In this section, you will see a model answer to help you understand how to structure a high-quality response. Then, you will have the opportunity to practise writing your own answer using a sample **Source 2.** Remember to ask your teacher for feedback!

The research claim is: *Screen time before going to sleep can negatively affect adolescents' academic performance.*

Source 2

Researchers conducted a true experiment to investigate whether screen use before bed has a negative impact on academic performance. Sixty high school students were randomly assigned to two groups:

- Group A used a screen for 45 minutes in bed before sleep.
- Group B read a book of their choice for 45 minutes before sleep.

Polysomnography (a tool to measure sleep) showed that Group A had delayed sleep onset and lower sleep-quality scores.

The next morning, participants completed a comprehension test with a score out of 10. Group A performed worse (median = 5) compared to Group B (median = 8) on the reading comprehension task. **Figure 1** shows the visual of the descriptive statistics. An independent t-test was applied to test the significance ($p = 0.00001$ at $p < 0.05$).

Figure 1

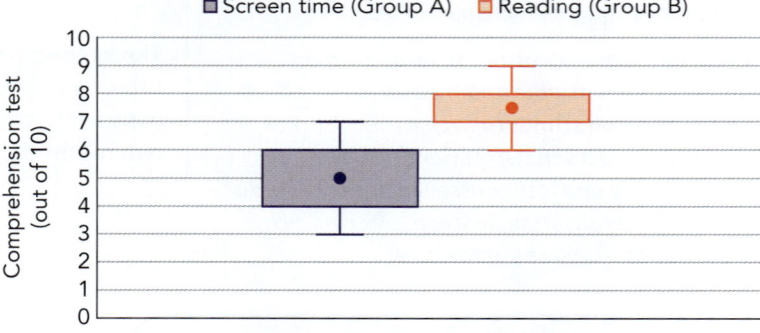

A graph comparing comprehension test performance between students who had screen time before sleep (Group A) and those who read a book (Group B)

2. Analyse the findings from **Source 2** and state a conclusion linked to the claim that screen time before going to bed can negatively affect adolescents' academic performance.

(6 marks)

Sample answer	Notes
The results show that students in the screen-use group (Group A) scored significantly lower on the comprehension test than those in Group B (reading group), as indicated by the difference in the descriptive statistics. The result was statistically significant (p < .00001), well below the conventional threshold of p < .05, allowing for the rejection of the null hypothesis. This suggests a real effect of screen use before sleep on next-day cognitive performance.	Accurate analysis of the inferential statistics provided.
*The box and whisker plot in **Figure 1** visually supports this finding, as the medians and interquartile ranges do not overlap, indicating a substantial performance gap between the two groups. Group A also showed greater variability, as seen in the wider spread of scores, which may reflect inconsistent effects of screen use on sleep quality and some variation between participants.*	Effective analysis of descriptive statistics and interpretation of the graph.
The measurement of sleep by Group A showed delayed sleep onset and lower sleep quality, which have been found to affect attention, memory and performance. The findings support the claim that screen time before bed may negatively impact adolescents' sleep and, in turn, affect academic performance.	The response ends with a clearly stated conclusion which is explicitly linked to the findings.

Now you try it

The research claim is: *Health and well-being mobile applications can improve student well-being.*

Source 2

A randomised controlled trial was conducted with 80 university students identified as having low well-being scores on the Warwick-Edinburgh Mental Wellbeing Scale (WEMWBS; 14 items, score range 14–70). Participants were randomly assigned to one of two groups using a matched pair design.
Pairs were formed on baseline WEMWBS score (± 2 points) before random allocation.

- Group A (n = 40) used a mindfulness app for 10 minutes each night for three weeks.

- Group B (n = 40) was placed on a waitlist and received no intervention.

All participants completed the WEMWBS before and after the intervention period. Higher scores on the scale (max = 70) indicate better mental well-being.

Table 1 presents descriptive statistics of post-intervention well-being scores.

Table 1

Group	Pre-test median	Pre-test IQR	Post-test median	Post-test IQR
Group A (mindfulness app)	39	3.0	53	4.0
Group B (waitlist)	39	3.0	40	3.0

The box and whiskers plot in **Figure 1** is based on the data in **Table 1**.

Figure 1

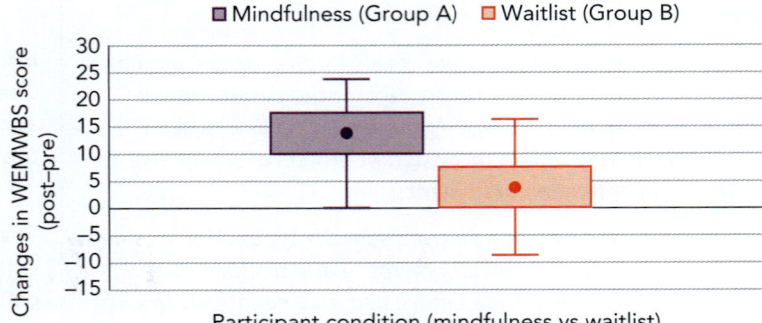

A graph to show the change in participant WEMWBS scores after a three-week mindfulness intervention (Group A) or no intervention on a waitlist (Group B)

■ Mindfulness (Group A)   ■ Waitlist (Group B)

Changes in WEMWBS score (post–pre)

Participant condition (mindfulness vs waitlist)

3. Analyse the findings from **Source 2** and state a conclusion linked to the claim that health and well-being mobile applications can improve student well-being.   **(6 marks)**

Health and well-being: Interviews

For the context Health and well-being, you need to be able to plan and conduct an **interview**. Interviews are an effective way in which to collect detailed thoughts and feelings from participants' experiences.

You can apply the key concepts in **Table 4.1** to interviews.

Concept	Application
Change	Interviews can capture personal experiences of health-related change. However, your class practicals are likely to be **cross-sectional** and not suited to tracking change over time.
Measurement	Reliable measurement in interviews depends on the creation of consistent, clear questions and careful **coding** to analyse open-ended responses.
Perspective	Interviews allow researchers to record a diverse range of perspectives, making them valuable for an in-depth understanding of personal and cultural perspectives on health and well-being.
Bias	Interviewer and response biases can distort data. However, training, neutral phrasing and multiple researchers can help reduce their impact.
Causality	Interviews can identify relationships between variables but cannot establish causation due to the lack of control over variables.
Responsibility	Researchers must ensure ethical conduct by protecting privacy, obtaining consent and handling sensitive health topics with care and cultural awareness.

Table 4.1: *The six key concepts and their application to interviews*

4.1 Introduction to interviews
Types of interviews

Health and well-being covers subjective topics, such as physical health and mental disorders, requiring a level of trust and rapport with participants.

Just as with other methods, researchers choose the type of interview that best fits the aims of their research. One important choice is whether to interview people one-on-one or in a group (called a **focus group**). If your aim is to explore *what* influences behaviour, then a **structured interview** may be best. If you are more focused on *why* behaviour changed, a **semi-structured interview** or focus group may be best.

Use the decision tree in **Figure 4.1** to help you decide which type of interview to use in your class practical.

Key concept: Causality

Interviews give insight into people's experiences, but they do not show cause and effect. For example, if someone says they feel stressed after moving to a new country, we cannot be sure the move *caused* the stress – there might be other factors involved. **Method triangulation** (combining with other methods) can help improve the **credibility**. Often, researchers pair interviews with another method.

Are you wanting to test a hypothesis or compare responses on what influences the behaviour? Do you have limited time for analysis?

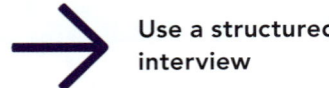 Use a structured interview

Are you wanting to explore topics with some flexibility to explore participants' unique experiences?

 Use a semi-structured interview

Are you wanting to explore group-based interactions and dynamics on a shared behaviour or experience? Or are you wanting to get multiple perspectives quickly?

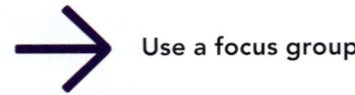 Use a focus group

Figure 4.1: Deciding which type of interview to use

You cannot use **unstructured interviews** for your class practical. They have no predetermined questions and are guided by the participant rather than the researcher, and so require highly skilled and trained interviewers.

Table 4.2 shows the differences between the different types of interviews you can undertake for your class practical.

Interview type	Description	For example...
Structured interview	Structured interviews are highly standardised interviews. They use a fixed set of questions that the interviewer asks using the same wording and in the same order for every participant. This consistency helps ensure **reliability** and makes the data easier to replicate and compare across participants. **A minimum of one participant is required.**	Interview of social media use and self-esteem Interview of exercise habits and mood
Semi-structured interview	Semi-structured interviews follow a general **interview guide** (questions or topics to be covered) but allow the interviewer to ask follow-up questions or adjust the order of questions based on the conversation. This approach offers a balance between structure and flexibility, helping researchers explore topics in more depth while still maintaining some level of consistency across interviews. **A minimum of one participant is required.**	Semi-structured interview with a school counsellor, fitness coach, yoga instructor and/or mindfulness practitioner
Focus group	Focus groups involve guided group discussions led by a facilitator, in which participants can respond to both the researcher and each other. They are especially useful for exploring shared experiences, such as how students perceive school food. The interaction between participants can generate rich insights, but responses may be influenced by group dynamics, and it can be challenging to separate individual viewpoints during analysis. **Between three and eight participants are required.**	How students manage their physical health or stress Students' perceptions of the effectiveness of mindfulness (Students can do a class practice of mindfulness first.)

Table 4.2: Different types of interviews and suggested practicals

Responsibility

Being an ethical researcher

When studying health and well-being, researchers have a responsibility to ensure participants are protected, respected and supported throughout the study. In line with IB ethical guidelines, you need to adhere to the following points in your class practical.

- **Respect for autonomy**: Participants must be informed about the topic and type of questions that will be asked. They must provide consent, especially if it involves mental health or discussing sensitive topics. Additionally, they need to be aware that they can withdraw and/or retract their data at any point during or after the study.

- **Minimising psychological harm**: You should not interview peers about personal or potentially distressing experiences, such as mental health concerns or bullying. More appropriate topics include stress management, healthy habits or media use. You must get approval from your teacher before undertaking the interview.

- **Confidentiality and anonymity**: Identities should be removed or hidden in transcripts and publications (anonymity), and any recordings should not be shared (confidentiality).

- **Cultural sensitivity**: Health and well-being are deeply shaped by culture and values. Researchers must avoid ethnocentrism and consider how cultural background affects participant understanding. This is especially relevant when exploring topics such as stigma, health beliefs or family dynamics.

- **Debriefing and support**: Participants must return to their original state at the end of the interview; this may require signposting to support services – for example, the school counsellor.

Study in focus

Lueck and Wilson (2010): How do social factors influence acculturative stress?

Lueck and Wilson's 2010 study aimed to investigate the factors that contribute to acculturative stress among Asian immigrants in the USA. Acculturative stress is the psychological strain that individuals experience when adjusting to a new culture while trying to maintain aspects of their original cultural identity. The study involved a total of 2095 Asian immigrants obtained through **stratified sampling**. They came from a range of ethnic backgrounds, including Chinese, Filipino, Vietnamese, Indian and others, representing a broad cross-section of the immigrant experience in the USA.

The researchers conducted semi-structured interviews with an interviewer with the same cultural and linguistic background, either face to face or via the internet. Interviews were translated and back translated to the initial language. Member checking took place with a randomly selected subset of participants who validated the data interpretation. The interviews focused on measuring acculturative stress and examining factors such as language proficiency, discrimination, family cohesion, social networks and socioeconomic status. Of the 2095 participants, 68 per cent (1433 participants) were found to experience acculturative stress based on their scores.

Key concept: Change

Interviews can be used to capture how people's thoughts and feelings change over time. The format allows for consistency in questioning (especially structured interviews), and any differences in responses across time points can reflect genuine behavioural change, rather than being dismissed as measurement error. This makes interviews a useful tool in **longitudinal** research on health and well-being.

The key findings included:

- Bilingualism and language preference: Participants who preferred speaking both their first language and English had lower acculturative stress, while those who only spoke in English experienced higher levels of stress.

- Discrimination: Experiences of prejudice and racial harassment were strongly linked to higher acculturative stress.

- Family and economic satisfaction: Strong family cohesion and satisfaction with economic opportunities in the USA were associated with lower acculturative stress.

Reflection

1. Why were semi-structured interviews useful in Lueck and Wilson's 2010 study of acculturative stress?

2. How did having the interviewer of the same background reduce bias?

3. What measures did the researchers take to ensure the findings of the study were credible?

4. What ethical considerations are there in Lueck and Wilson's 2010 study?

Lueck, K. and Wilson, M. (2010). Acculturative stress in Asian immigrants: The impact of social and linguistic factors. *International Journal of Intercultural Relations, 34*(1), 47–57.

Planning an interview

A good interview needs structure. Using an interview guide, with a list of questions or topics to cover, will help you maintain your focus and consistency across interviews. Your questions should be **open-ended**, which means they will invite the participant to elaborate on their answers, rather than simply saying 'yes' or 'no'.

- For a 30-minute interview, you should aim for 6–8 core questions.
- For a 60-minute interview, you should aim for 10–12 core questions.

You should use a variety of question types in your interview guide to elicit responses from participants:

- Descriptive questions invite the participant to describe events or experiences.
- Structural questions explore underlying meanings and personal definitions.
- Contrast questions encourage comparison between experiences or choices.
- Evaluative questions ask for feelings, opinions or personal judgements.

Conducting a **pilot test** will help to ensure your wording is clear, questions are the right length and that you have covered all intended themes. It is a good idea to trial your interview questions with a teacher or peer, note any points of confusion and revise your interview guide based on their feedback.

It is important to keep your facial expressions and body language neutral during the interview, and to listen fully to the participant with the goal of understanding their viewpoint. This is known as **active listening**. This can reduce **interviewer**

effects where the interviewer's behaviour, appearance or attitudes influence how participants respond. For example, participants might respond differently depending on the gender of the interviewer, which could lead to bias.

It is important to consider how you will record participants' answers. Taking notes can lead to details being missed and interrupt the flow of the conversation. Therefore, researchers often use audio or video recordings (with consent). Afterwards, you will transcribe verbatim (word for word) what participants said, often with comments on their tone, pauses and facial expressions. The length of your interview is important as this will affect how long it takes to undertake transcription and **thematic analysis**.

Activity 1: Practising open-ended questions

Identify the question type being used in each of the following open-ended interview questions on social media and self-esteem.

1. 'You mentioned feeling "less successful" after using social media. Can you explain what that means to you?'

2. 'Can you tell me about a time when scrolling through social media affected how you saw yourself?'

3. 'How do you feel about the way in which social media influences your self-esteem?'

4. 'How do you think comparing yourself to people on social media is different from comparing yourself to classmates in real life?'

Bonus: Write four additional questions for this interview guide. Try to include all four types of questions.

Compare and contrast It!: Paper 2 Question 1c
Interviews versus other research methods

Paper 2 Section A Question **1c** will ask you to compare and contrast your interview with another research method. You have already compared the use of interviews with surveys (section 2.1) and experiments (section 3.1). Use **Table 4.3** to help plan your response for other research methods.

Remember that in the exam you will need to discuss each similarity and difference in detail. For example:

Interviews focus on gaining insight into personal perspectives and lived experiences, while experiments are designed to identify causal relationships. Interviews offer flexibility and can be conducted in naturalistic settings, which enhances ecological validity. In contrast, experiments take place in controlled environments to minimise confounding variables. This reflects different priorities in psychological research – interviews value depth and context, whereas experiments prioritise control and replicability.

Similarities	Differences
Interviews vs observations	
• Both methods involve a structured approach to data collection, using tools including interview guides or observation checklists to maintain consistency and enable replication. • They both primarily gather **qualitative** data and aim to explore patterns or relationships between variables. However, they do not establish causality. • Credibility is essential: techniques like member checking and **triangulation** can be used. For more information on observations, see Chapter 5.	• Interviews depend heavily on participants being open and willing to share, whereas observations rely on capturing naturally occurring behaviour. • Interviews focus on gathering personal insights and self-reported experiences, while observations aim to record the frequency and nature of behaviour as it happens. • Interviews offer more flexibility, allowing for follow-up questions. Observations are often more rigidly structured.
Interviews vs case studies	
• Both gather rich, qualitative data to explore complex psychological phenomena. • Both often involve in-depth investigation of individuals or small groups. • Both require ethical awareness and **reflexivity** due to the personal nature of the data. For more information on case studies, see Chapter 1.	• Interviews are a method of data collection, whereas case studies are a broader research strategy. • Case studies may include multiple methods (for example, interviews, observations, documents), while interviews are standalone. • Interviews can involve many participants, while case studies usually focus on a single participant or the same group of participants.
Interviews vs correlational studies	
• Both explore relationships between variables without manipulating them, but do not establish causality. • Both can be used in naturalistic settings, making them suitable for real-world research. • Both can gather **quantitative** data (structured interview). For more information on correlational studies, see Chapter 1.	• Interviews collect qualitative data, while correlational studies use quantitative data. • Correlational studies can analyse large samples statistically, whereas interviews focus on depth with fewer participants. • Correlational studies can identify associations, while interviews explore subjective interpretations of experiences.

Table 4.3: The similarities and differences between interviews and other research methods

4.2 Structured interviews

A structured interview involves a structured approach. The interviewer follows a fixed set of predetermined questions that they ask in a specific order. They do not deviate from the interview guide. Unlike semi-structured or unstructured interviews, structured interviews contain the exact same questions in each interview, making the data more standardised and easier to compare across participants.

Structured interviews are well-suited for studies exploring health and well-being, as the consistent format allows researchers to identify patterns across participants and to make comparisons across social and cultural groups. Additionally, the use of standardised tools, such as the Beck Depression Inventory (BDI) – a self-scoring tool – can be administered as a structured interview, which provides a way of objectively studying subjective behaviours.

There are strengths and limitations of using structured interviews (**Table 4.4**).

> **Key concept: Measurement**
>
> Structured interviews often have **test–retest reliability**. In structured interviews, using identical questions can help researchers see whether participants' responses remain stable or show meaningful changes – for example, in a study on self-esteem before and after a break from social media. High test–retest reliability means the tool is dependable for tracking changes over time.

Strengths	Limitations
Standardised questions: They are easier to code and analyse, allowing comparisons, which increases the reliability.	**Limited depth**: The rigid structure can mean information is missed when exploring personal topics and experiences.
Not as time consuming: They are quicker to conduct and analyse than other types of interviews, which is useful in health and well-being research that utilises a large sample.	**Limited flexibility**: If interesting points are made, the researcher cannot probe and ask follow-up questions.
Reduces interviewer bias: The structured format minimises the interviewer's influence, ensuring data remains objective.	**Limited rapport**: Participants may feel restricted by the fixed questions, especially when discussing sensitive health topics, which could lead to under-reporting.

Table 4.4: The strengths and limitations of structured interviews

4.3 Semi-structured interviews

Perspective

In a semi-structured interview, the researcher has a set of predetermined questions and a degree of flexibility to explore topics in more detail based on the participant's responses. The interviewer can follow an interview guide but also probe, ask follow-up questions or address topics that arise organically in the conversation. It combines the reliability of a structured interview with the flexibility of an unstructured interview.

> **Key concept: Perspective**
>
> **Positivist methods** (for example, structured interviews) aim to measure variables objectively, while **interpretivist methods** (for example, semi-structured interviews) seek to understand participants' subjective meanings.

Semi-structured interviews are particularly valuable in studying health and well-being because they allow researchers to explore deeply personal and often complex topics. Building a rapport (trusting relationship) with the participant is essential in this type of interview – the more comfortable the participant, the more likely they will be to share their honest experiences.

Study in focus

Brown and Harris (1978): Factors influencing the onset of depression

Brown and Harris (1978) conducted a groundbreaking study into the link between life events and the onset of depression in women. They created the Life Events and Difficulties Schedule (LEDS) – a semi-structured interview guide to study life stressors – and interviewed 458 women in London to assess recent life stressors and contextual factors.

The researchers found that women who had experienced a severe life event or difficulty were significantly more vulnerable to developing depression, especially when combined with factors such as lack of social support, early loss of a parent or having young children. The study highlighted the social origins of depression and the value of in-depth interviews in understanding risk factors for mental health. It is important to note that the life events were self-reported, which may introduce bias into the study – such as recall bias – and the specific sample could raise questions about generalisability.

Brown, G. W. and Harris, T. (1978). *Social origins of depression: A study of psychiatric disorder in women*. Tavistock.

Reflection

Using Brown and Harris's 1978 study, create a table of the strengths and limitations of semi-structured interviews in the topic of health and well-being.

Consider and include the following points.

- Time needed
- Flexibility
- Interviewer bias
- Rich data
- Reliability
- Rapport
- Trained interviewers

4.4 Focus groups

A focus group involves a guided group discussion on a specific topic. Typically, it involves 6–10 participants sharing their views in a semi-structured discussion led by a facilitator. However, the IB guidelines stipulate 3–8 participants for your class practical. The facilitators' role is to introduce the group and the topic, to keep the conversation focused and to ensure participants' participation. Participants build on each other's ideas, offering deeper insights, which yields rich data. You can gain a lot more valuable data in a short period of time, but transcribing this can often be more challenging.

When researching health and well-being, focus groups are especially useful for exploring shared experiences, social dynamics and group beliefs.

Key concept: Bias

In focus groups, one or two participants might dominate the conversation. This is known as **dominant responder bias**. This can skew the data, limiting the range of perspectives and reducing the credibility of findings. Using skilled researchers, establishing ground rules and inclusive questioning are crucial considerations to minimise this bias.

Activity 2: When to use a focus group

Focus groups can be a rich source of data, offering natural interaction and a wide range of perspectives. Participants can reflect on and build upon each other's responses, which can deepen insights. However, they are not always a suitable method, especially for sensitive topics, where concerns about confidentiality and social desirability may reduce participants' responses.

A key concern is dominant responder bias, where one or more outspoken participants dominate the conversation. This can discourage quieter individuals from contributing, skew the discussion toward the dominant viewpoint, and ultimately reduce the diversity and balance of perspectives in the data.

Additionally, researchers have less control over the discussion compared to individual interviews, which can lead to off-topic dialogue and make analysis more challenging. These factors can affect both the ethical integrity of the study and the quality of the findings, and should be carefully considered when choosing focus groups as a research method.

For each of the health and well-being research questions listed:

- Decide whether a focus group is appropriate for the research question, and provide justification for your decision.
- If *not*, what alternative interview or method might be better suited?

Research questions

1. How do high school students manage their stress during exam periods?
2. What are young people's views on body image and social media?
3. How do adolescents perceive vaping and its risks?
4. What barriers do students with eating disorders face in accessing mental health support?
5. How does participation in team sports impact the well-being of students?

Responsibility: Being an ethical researcher

In addition to the main ethical considerations, focus groups need to adhere to the following additional considerations.

- **Confidentiality**: While the researcher can protect data confidentiality, they cannot guarantee that the other group members will keep information private.

  Solution: Remind participants not to share what is discussed beyond the group. It is considered good practice to have participants sign a confidentiality agreement.

- **Anonymity**: True anonymity is difficult as participants see and hear each other.

  Solution: Ask participants to use only their initials to introduce themselves.

- **Sensitive topics**: If you are discussing personal issues, participants may feel vulnerable.

  Solution: Create a safe space and set clear ground rules – for example, respect, no interruptions and the use of sensitive language.

- **Group dynamics**: Be aware of dominant responders who may influence others or suppress differing views.

  Solution: You need to manage the discussion to ensure equal participation.

4.5 Analysing interview data

All of you need to know how to analyse interviews, to learn core analysis skills. However, **only HL students** will be assessed on data interpretation and analysis (in Paper 3).

In this section, you will discover how to undertake thematic analysis, the importance of reflexivity and how to increase credibility and **transferability**. If you are an HL student, there are practice questions for you to try in section 4.8.

Thematic analysis

Researchers use thematic analysis to analyse qualitative data in order to identify, analyse and report patterns (themes) within data. They use it to analyse interview transcripts, observation notes, questionnaire responses or other textual data sources. Thematic analysis is particularly useful in health and well-being studies as it allows researchers to interpret the lived experiences, thoughts and feelings of participants.

Unlike quantitative methods, thematic analysis does not rely on numerical data. Instead, it emphasises meaning-making and interpretation. Meaning-making in interviews refers to how participants express and interpret the personal significance of their experiences, allowing researchers to understand not just what happened, but what it meant to the individual. The method helps researchers answer questions about how people perceive and make sense of their experiences.

The six steps of thematic analysis

Figure 4.2 summarises the six steps of thematic analysis outlined by Braun and Clarke (2006).

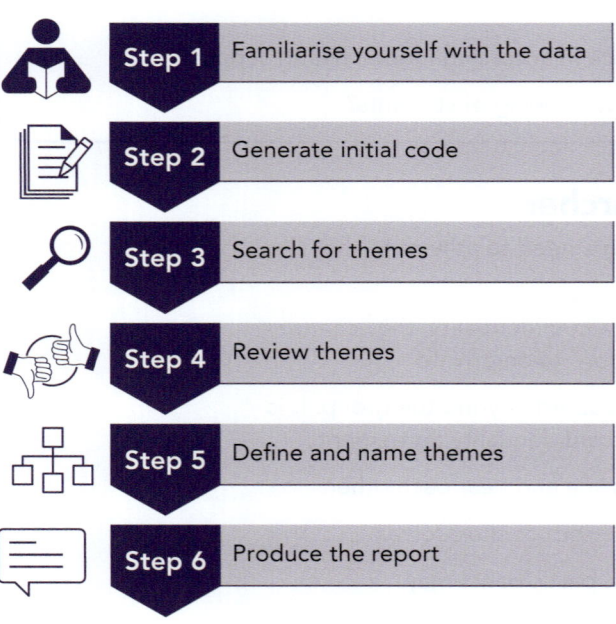

Step 1 — Familiarise yourself with the data
Step 2 — Generate initial code
Step 3 — Search for themes
Step 4 — Review themes
Step 5 — Define and name themes
Step 6 — Produce the report

Figure 4.2: The process of thematic analysis

> **Key concept: Bias**
>
> Reflexivity is an ongoing process in which researchers reflect on their background and beliefs and how these may influence their research. In thematic analysis, it is important for researchers to reflect on how their own beliefs, experiences and assumptions may influence how they interpret the data. **Researcher triangulation** (the use of more than one researcher) in the interpretation can reduce bias and improve the consistency between researchers (**inter-rater reliability**).

Example

Imagine you have completed the following research.

- Aim: To explore the motivational barriers to exercise experienced by female secondary school teachers

- Interview research question: What role does motivation play in female secondary school teachers' exercise habits?

- Interview type: Structured interview

- Sample: 12 female secondary school teachers

- Interviewee: Secondary school teacher (female, age 27 years)

Your next task is to analyse your interview transcripts.

Steps 1 and 2: Familiarise yourself with the data and generate initial code. Read and re-read your transcripts. Begin noting down your initial observations and any patterns you see. For example:

Interviewer: Can you describe your current exercise habits?

mental clarity   *daily light exercise*

Participant: *'I try to walk at least 30 minutes every day, usually after school. It helps me clear my head. But during busy weeks – when reports are due, lots of parent meetings – it's easy to skip. I used to go to the gym…erm, but now I find it hard to motivate myself after a long day.'*

motivation   *work-life balance*

Interviewer: What effect does exercise have on your mood?

improved emotions

Participant: *'Oh, uh….it definitely makes a difference. I'm more…patient with students, and I sleep better. If I miss too many days, I start feeling…well…irritable or anxious. It's like my reset button.'*

emotional reset   *negative effects on mood*

Steps 3–5: Search, review, define and name themes. During these steps, you organise the codes into potential themes, based on the patterns you see. Then you review these themes and check how well they reflect the data. At this point, you may decide to merge, divide or even discard some themes. You then clearly define the remaining themes and give them concise, informative names based on a key pattern you found in the data that is important to your research. For example:

- *Routine and habits* (for example, *daily light exercise*)

- *Psychological benefits* (for example, *mental clarity, emotional reset*)

- *Emotional effects* (for example, *negative effects on mood, improved emotions*)

- *Barriers to being active* (for example, *work-life balance, motivation*)

Step 6: Produce the report. Use the themes to inform your narrative and use direct quotes from your thematic analysis of your interview transcript. For example:

The data suggests that the participant uses light physical activity as a psychological regulation strategy to manage work-related stress. However, time and reduced energy are mentioned as barriers to sustaining this. The theme, 'recovery through routine', was supported by references to walking, running and yoga as grounding techniques.

Activity 3: Practising thematic analysis

Objective: You will apply the six steps of Braun and Clarke's (2006) thematic analysis to your own transcript from the interview or focus group you conducted in the class practical.

Step 1: Transcribe and highlight key ideas. Listen to the audio of your interview or focus group, or re-read your notes, and transcribe one short section (3–5 minutes). As you read your transcript, highlight or underline key phrases that stand out – those that are interesting or repeated, or seem significant.

Steps 2–5: Code and group into themes. Annotate your transcript. Write short labels (codes) beside any phrases that you identified in Step 1. Then look for codes that relate to each other and group them into themes.

Researcher triangulation: Swap your themes with a partner and give feedback, considering the following aspects.

- Are the codes relevant? Did they miss any significant parts in the transcript?
- Are the themes accurate and meaningful? Do any need to be merged, divided or discarded?

Make revisions, then answer the following reflection questions.

Reflection

1. What are the key findings and conclusions of your study?
2. What have you learned about the process of thematic analysis, and how helpful do you find this technique in understanding participants' experiences of health and well-being?
3. How could your study be evaluated in terms of sample, design and data collection?

HL Credibility, bias, transferability

Paper 3 Question 3 asks you to discuss a qualitative source in terms of *credibility*, *bias* and *transferability*. It is important to discuss both the steps taken and how the actions of the researcher could improve the research findings.

Credibility

Credibility refers to the extent to which the findings of a qualitative study can be trusted as an accurate reflection of the participants' experiences. This can include:

- **Member checking**: This is often referred to as credibility checking. It involves asking the participants to review the themes and interpretations to ensure they align with their actual experiences.
- **Document**: Keep a record (trail) of your documentation on how you identified themes.

- **Inter-coder reliability**: Use multiple researchers to code and identify themes to ensure consistency and reduce bias in theme identification.
- **Reflexivity**: Reflect on your own assumptions and biases.
- **Data or method triangulation**: Use data from different sources or methods to cross-check the findings.
- **Thick descriptions**: Provide detailed quotes and rich descriptions to support themes.

Bias

Bias refers to any systematic distortion in the research process that can affect the accuracy or objectivity of findings. In qualitative research, it is possible to introduce bias during data collection, interpretation or analysis.

You have already reviewed how reflexivity and researcher triangulation can reduce researcher bias. Interviewer training and standardised procedures can also help establish consistency in how interviews are conducted.

Transferability

Transferability in qualitative research refers to the extent to which the findings of a study can be applied or generalised to other contexts, settings or groups beyond the original sample. This can include:

- **Contextual details**: Provide thick descriptions of the context of the interview/focus group to allow others to evaluate the relevance in different settings.
- **Sample characteristics**: Describe the demographic characteristics of the sample to assess how the findings might apply to other populations.
- **Comparison with existing research**: Compare your findings and highlight common themes or differences. This is where your knowledge of motivation, culture and technology come in handy!

Remember that you need to discuss what has been considered already and further considerations, with each point linking to the source.

Reflection activity

Consider surveys/questionnaires, experiments and interviews/focus groups when answering this question:

1. How might researchers avoid bias and ensure trustworthy interpretations (credibility)?

Hint: Think about bias in participant responses, research methods and/or the researchers.

4.6 Class practical planning worksheet
Interviews

This worksheet will help you prepare for Paper 2 Section A Question 1. A blank version can be downloaded from collins.co.uk/internationalresources. Ensure that you design and record your class practical clearly enough to use as the basis for the exam. You can record your answers in a copy of the *Class practical recording sheet* (refer to Chapter 1). An idea for your class practical could be to explore how students manage their physical health or stress.

Aim and research question

What is the aim of your investigation?	*Consider the part of health and well-being that you want to understand.*
What is the specific issue or problem you are exploring? Have you conducted background research on this issue?	
Why is this worth exploring in your school or community context?	*Think about whether this class practical could link to a CAS project.*

Research methodology

Which type of interview will you conduct, and why?	*Consider how far you want comparison between participant responses (structured), an in-depth understanding of participant perspectives (semi-structured), or whether a group setting will make participants more comfortable sharing (focus group).*
What are the key themes or areas your questions will explore?	
What sampling method will you use (for example, opportunity, purposive)? Why is this sampling method appropriate?	
Who is your target population? What sample size are you aiming for?	*You need a minimum of one for structured or semi-structured interviews, and between three and eight for a focus group. Consider what is important when selecting students (for example, diversity of perspectives).*
Which specific ethical considerations are needed for the interview?	*Think about how you will inform participants of their rights, including anonymity, confidentiality, informed consent and the right to withdraw.*

Data collection

Which type of questions will you ask? How many questions will there be in your interview schedule?	*Try to plan the types of questions you will ask, as well as follow-up or probing questions to help you go deeper. You may also need to ensure that you standardise your questions across participants.*
How will you phrase questions to avoid bias?	*Consider ways to avoid bias in your own questions, and reducing dominant responder bias.*
How will you record and transcribe the responses?	*If you are recording audio, you need to ask for consent to record.*
Which key concepts are relevant to your practical, and why?	

Data analysis

How will you organise and analyse your qualitive data to identify patterns or themes?	
How will you use a framework like Braun and Clarke's (2006) thematic analysis?	
How will you ensure your interpretation is credible?	

Discussion

What are the main threats to validity or reliability?	
How could bias potentially affect the credibility of your research?	*Could participants try to give 'acceptable' answers? How far is the sample going to be representative of the population of interest?*
How could your findings be applied in real-life settings? Consider both short-term applications (immediate use in schools) and long-term applications (for example, policy changes).	*Consider ways in which your class practical could inform well-being initiatives or strategies that individuals could use.*

4.7 Apply it! Paper 2 practice questions

Section A Question **1d** requires you to design your study using a different method. It is important to explain the procedure in detail and apply key terminology.

Imagine you have conducted semi-structured interviews exploring student perceptions of how mindfulness before assessments can lower academic stress.

1d. Design an experiment to investigate the same topic as you studied in your class practical. **(6 marks)**

Sample answer	Notes
A true experiment could be undertaken using an independent measures design to investigate the effect of mindfulness on academic stress. Participants could be randomly allocated to either the mindfulness intervention group (experimental group) or no intervention (control group). The independent variable would be whether participants engaged with a mindfulness exercise before a test, and the dependent variable would be the reported stress levels after a test.	
The intervention group would complete a five-minute guided breathing exercise using a recorded script via headphones to ensure standardisation. The other group would sit in silence for the same amount of time with no recording. Immediately after, all participants would complete 10 trivia questions on an answer paper with a three-minute timer, followed by six Likert questions measuring their stress levels (for example, 'I felt calm entering the test').	The description of the procedure is accurate, showing knowledge and understanding of the research method provided.

Sample answer	Notes
All instructions would be the same and there would be control over confounding variables, such as the time of day or noise. To avoid researcher bias, the study could be single-blind, with students unaware of the full aim. No identifying data would be collected to maintain confidentiality. Ethical guidelines such as informed consent would be followed. Although stress induced is minimal and temporary, the debriefing could provide information about academic well-being resources.	Terminology relating to true experiments is used effectively throughout the response.

Now you try it

Practice these Paper 2 Section A questions based on your interview class practical. You could try them in timed conditions, in which case, only give yourself 50 minutes. Remember to ask your teacher for feedback!

1a. Describe how you used an interview in your class practical, including the aim and procedure. **(4 marks)**

1b. Explain the concept of bias in relation to your interview or focus group class practical. **(4 marks)**

1c. Compare and contrast the use of an interview used in your class practical with an experiment. **(6 marks)**

1d. Design a survey/questionnaire to investigate the same topic as you investigated in your class practical. **(6 marks)**

HL 4.8 Apply it! HL focus

Paper 3 Question 3 requires you to consider qualitative research in terms of *credibility*, *bias* or *transferability*. The question will refer to a study described in **Source 3**, which will be provided in a separate Resource Booklet during the exam. You will be asked **one** of the following questions based on that source.

- Discuss how the researcher could improve the credibility of the findings.

- Discuss how the researcher could avoid bias.

- To what extent are the findings transferable to other populations or contexts?

In this section, you will see a model answer to help you understand how to structure a high-quality response. Then you will have the opportunity to practise writing your own answer using a sample **Source 3**. Remember to ask your teacher for feedback!

The research claim is: *Screen time before going to sleep can negatively affect adolescents' academic performance.*

Source 3

A researcher conducted 12 semi-structured interviews with female students aged 15–16 years from one urban upper-secondary school in a large metropolitan city. The aim of the study was to explore students' experiences of screen time and sleep. The researcher used thematic analysis and identified three themes:

- Students reported staying up late, often endlessly scrolling through social media content ('doom scrolling') on their phones, and viewed this as a problem.

- Students struggled to maintain a consistent sleep routine due to workload and the number of distractions.

- There was an awareness that screen time affects their sleep quality.

3. Discuss how the researcher could avoid bias. **(6 marks)**

Sample answer	Notes
In qualitative research, minimising bias is essential to improve credibility and ensure the findings represent participants' perspectives.	The definition shows understanding of the research consideration.
One way the researcher can avoid bias is by using a well-piloted semi-structured interview schedule. This ensures that participants are asked the same non-leading questions, reducing interviewer bias. Furthermore, the use of open-ended questions, such as 'What does your bedtime routine look like?', supports more authentic responses and limits response bias.	The first point made relates to reducing bias in the method.
To reduce confirmation bias during analysis, the researcher should employ reflexivity, reflecting on how their own identity may bring bias into the research – for example, being female or having a connection to the school. Keeping a reflexive diary helps to create an audit trail that external examiners can check.	The second section discusses reducing bias in the researcher.
Another way to reduce this would be to check for inter-coder reliability, where a second researcher independently reviews and codes the transcripts and agreement is calculated (for example, Cohen's $\kappa \geq 0.80$). This would ensure that themes, such as the 'doom scrolling', are grounded in the data rather than the primary researcher's expectations.	
Finally, the researcher could apply member checking, where they could share the preliminary themes with participants to confirm whether they accurately represented their views. For example, students could verify whether the theme of a lack of consistent sleep routines truly reflected their lived experience. This helps confirm accuracy and reduces researcher bias.	The final point relates to reducing bias in the participants.
Taken together, a piloted schedule, reflexive practice, inter-coder reliability and member-checking would maximise the study's credibility and minimise bias.	All points are linked consistently to the stimulus. The final sentence offers a succinct summary of the points made.

Now you try it

The research claim is: *Health and well-being mobile applications can improve student well-being.*

Source 3

A focus group with eight IB DP students aimed to explore how using technology-based mindfulness affected their emotional well-being. Before the focus group, students downloaded the mindfulness app and watched a mindfulness video followed by a practice session each day for one week. From the thematic analysis, the research identified the following themes.

- Students found the apps helped provide a structure and guidance for practising mindfulness.
- Having the app on their phone helped them form a habit and reminded them to do mindfulness sessions.
- Using the mindfulness app helped them feel calmer.
- Mindfulness was particularly useful in the morning and helped with mental clarity.

3. Discuss how the researcher could improve the credibility of the findings.

(6 marks)

Human development: Observation

For the context Human development, you need to be able to plan and conduct an **observation**. Observations are used when it is not practical or ethical to study certain behaviours in controlled settings, such as infant attachment or peer interactions.

You can apply the key concepts in **Table 5.1** to observations.

Concept	Application
Bias	Bias can arise from the researcher, which can distort how behaviour is recorded, while participant **reactivity** may alter participants' natural responses. Using coding systems can improve **inter-rater reliability**.
Causality	**Longitudinal** observation captures developmental changes over time. Observations can show correlations and patterns, but cannot establish cause-and-effect due to a lack of control. Longitudinal research can offer stronger support for causal inferences than **cross-sectional** observations.
Change	Observations are well-suited to tracking developmental changes over time. Consistent settings and procedures are essential to capturing change accurately.
Measurement	Valid measurement requires clear definitions of behaviours and standardised tools. Calculate inter-rater reliability to quantify agreement.
Perspective	Cultural and theoretical perspectives influence how observers interpret behaviour. Including diverse viewpoints can provide a more balanced understanding. Compare etic (outsider) and emic (insider) interpretations of behaviour. For example, an outsider (etic) might interpret a toddler crying as manipulation, while a parent (emic) might see it as distress.
Responsibility	Ethical considerations are vital when observing children, including informed consent from parents/guardians, confidentiality and minimising harm.

Table 5.1: The six key concepts and their application to observations

5.1 Introduction to observations
Why are observations useful?

Observations are particularly useful in studying human development because they allow researchers to go beyond what participants *say* and gain valuable insight into what they actually *do*. This method is often used when psychologists aim to study behaviour as it occurs naturally, without manipulating variables or intruding on participants' behaviour.

Study in focus

Fagot (1978): Gender-typed behaviours

Fagot (1978) conducted a structured, non-participant, **naturalistic observation** of 24 families with toddlers aged 20–24 months to investigate how parents reinforce gender-typed behaviours. Observations were conducted in families' homes using a behavioural checklist of pre-defined gendered behaviours (for example, throwing a ball or playing with dolls). Each child was observed for five 60-second periods across several sessions.

Findings showed parents reacted more positively when children engaged in behaviours aligned with their perceived gender norms (for example, girls showing dependence, boys being active) and more negatively when children displayed cross-gender behaviour – particularly when girls engaged in physically active play. A follow-up survey found that parents were unaware of these biases, as their self-reported attitudes did not match their observed behaviour. The study highlights how gender role **enculturation** begins early in development and is reinforced by parents.

Reflection

1. Why was the follow-up survey with parents useful, and how does it support the use of observation in Fagot's (1978) study?

2. What ethical considerations does the study raise about studying human development with children?

Fagot, B.I. (1978). The influence of sex of child on parental reactions to toddler children. *Child development, 49(2), 459.*

Designing an observation

Once you have identified your research question, the next step is to design your observation. You need **at least one participant** for your observation. There are several decisions you need to make when designing your observation, which will influence how you collect data and how you analyse it. The initial decision needs are based on:

- how you structure the observation
- the setting you choose for the observation
- whether the participants will be aware that they are being observed
- your role as the researcher during the observation.

Table 5.2 provides an overview of the factors you will need to consider in the design of your observation. They are explained in more detail in section 5.2.

Factor	Option 1	Option 2	Consideration
Structure	Structured	Unstructured	Do you already know the behaviours you want to observe? Do you want to gather qualitative or quantitative data?

Factor	Option 1	Option 2	Consideration
Setting	Naturalistic	Controlled	Do you want to study natural behaviour, or do you want to standardise the setting, allowing for easier comparison?
Participant awareness	Overt	Covert	To what extent will participants change their behaviour if they know they are being observed? Does this affect your research aim?
Role of researcher	Participant	Non-participant	To what extent will you need to remain objective?

Table 5.2: Factors to consider when designing an observation

Another consideration is deciding how behaviour will be recorded in an observation. There are three main techniques used by researchers:

- **Time sampling:** The researcher records behaviour at fixed time intervals (for example, every 30 seconds or 5 minutes), which can be efficient for longer observations as it captures general patterns. This can reduce observer fatigue; however, the researcher may miss behaviours between the intervals.

- **Point sampling:** Observations are made of one individual at a specific moment in time, often rotating between individuals. This allows detailed focus on individual behaviour across a group.

- **Event sampling:** This is commonly used in structured observations in which every occurrence of a specific pre-planned behaviour is recorded during the observation period. This allows a clear focus to the data collection; however, it can require more attention by the researcher.

Compare and contrast It!: Paper 2 Question 1c
Observations versus other research methods

Paper 2 Section A Question **1c** will ask you to compare and contrast your observation with another research method. You have already compared the use of observations with surveys (section 2.1), experiments (section 3.1) and interview (section 4.1). Use **Table 5.3** to help plan your response for other research methods.

Remember that in the exam you will need to discuss each similarity and difference in detail. For example:

Observations and interviews are both qualitative methods used to understand human behaviour in natural contexts. They are often conducted in real-life settings and aim to collect rich, in-depth data. Both can be structured or unstructured, offering flexibility based on the research goal, and focus on behaviour as it naturally occurs rather than manipulating variables. However, they differ in data collection: observations record behaviour, while interviews explore participants' thoughts and experiences. Also, interviews involve face-to-face interaction, which can introduce bias, whereas covert observations reduce reactivity but raise ethical concerns, such as the lack of informed consent.

Similarities	Differences
Observations vs case studies	
<ul><li>Both offer **holistic** insights into behaviour and are frequently used to gain context-rich data.</li><li>Both can explore groups of people's behaviour in depth.</li><li>Both prioritise rich, contextual detail, which is often used in exploratory or descriptive research.</li></ul> For more information on case studies, see Chapter 1.	<ul><li>Case studies often use multiple data collection methods (method triangulation), whereas observations are usually standalone methods.</li><li>Case studies focus on a single individual or small group in depth, but observations can involve broader participant groups.</li><li>Observations typically focus on present behaviour, whereas case studies can include retrospective data and longitudinal analysis.</li></ul>
Observations vs correlational studies	
<ul><li>Both are non-experimental methods and cannot demonstrate causality.</li><li>Both can be conducted in natural environments, increasing ecological validity.</li><li>Both are useful for exploring relationships between naturally occurring variables.</li></ul> For more information on correlational studies, see Chapter 1.	<ul><li>Observations can be quantitative or qualitative, whereas correlational studies require only quantitative data.</li><li>Observations capture natural behaviour, but correlational studies often use self-reported or existing data.</li><li>Observations focus on what is seen, while correlational studies focus on statistical associations between variables across participants.</li></ul>

Table 5.3: The similarities and differences between observations and other research methods

Responsibility

Being an ethical researcher

When studying human development, researchers have a responsibility to ensure participants are protected, respected and supported throughout the study. In line with IB ethical guidelines, you need to adhere to the following points in your class practical.

- **Consent:** Remember that participants under the age of 16 years require written permission from a parent or guardian. You will also need the consent from the teachers responsible for different year groups.

- **Naturalistic observations:** Researchers must balance ethical responsibilities with the goal of capturing authentic behaviour. Gaining consent beforehand can lead to reactivity, where participants alter their behaviour because they know they are being observed. To avoid this, researchers may choose covert observation, where consent is not obtained in advance. In some cases, such as observing in public spaces (for example, parks or shopping centres) where people generally expect to be seen, prior consent may not be required. Note that a classroom setting is not defined as a public setting and consent is required.

- **Anonymity and confidentiality:** You must ensure that no names or identifying information are recorded or shared. You can only record the observation itself, provided you have consent from the participants. You must keep all data confidential, ensuring that it is only used for the class practical and is deleted afterwards.

- **Restrictions:** You cannot use animals or conduct any conformity/obedience studies. Covert participant observations are also prohibited for class practicals.

5.2 Planning your observation

When planning your class practical observation, you need to consider the length of the observation. Remember: the longer the observation, the more data you have to analyse! You are advised to restrict your class practical observation to 20 minutes, as this will give you enough time to observe the behaviour.

You also need to carefully consider the structure of your observation, the setting, whether the participant(s) will be aware of your presence and your role as the researcher.

Structure: Structured vs unstructured

A **structured observation**, often known as a systematic observation, uses a pre-prepared checklist of the behaviours that researchers expect to see based on their hypothesis or existing research. The researcher counts the frequency of the behaviour using the checklist. This **deductive approach** can yield consistent data, which is easier to analyse. However, it can limit what is noticed, as it's based on pre-set categories.

If you choose a structured observation, a **coding scheme** (a pre-set list of behaviours to tick) helps organise and analyse the behaviour consistently. Coding schemes can be broad or specific. For a 20-minute observation, you should aim for between five and 10 codes. A **pilot** observation is useful for identifying and refining behavioural codes before the main study.

> **Key concept: Measurement**
>
> A structured approach supports valid measurement by ensuring that the behaviours recorded are clearly operationalised. A coding scheme with clear definitions can reduce bias and improve inter-rater reliability.

Table 5.4 provides an example of the different types of coding schemes for a study on student engagement in a classroom.

Coding scheme	Focus	Example
Macroanalytic	Broad categories of behaviour	Group discussion in a lesson
Microanalytic	Small, specific actions	A student asks a question
Mesoanalytic	A mix of broad and specific categories of behaviours	Opportunities for group discussion and how many students contribute

Table 5.4: Different types of coding schemes

The number of times the behaviour occurs is recorded in a **frequency table** (**Table 5.5**).

Behaviour observed	Frequency
Group discussion in a lesson	3
Student asks a question	5
Opportunities for group discussion and how many students contribute	12 (4)

Table 5.5: Frequency table

An **unstructured observation**, also referred to as an unsystematic observation, does not use a coding scheme and is more flexible in the recording of behaviour. Instead, researchers write down everything during or immediately after the observation; these are known as **field notes**. This **inductive approach** generates qualitative data and is especially useful when little is known about the behaviour being studied or when exploring a new research area. Typically, notes will include a detailed description of the behaviour, interactions, context and the researcher's reflections.

Table 5.6 summarises the strengths and limitations of structured and unstructured observations.

Observation type	Strengths	Limitations
Structured	<ul><li>Easy to compare and analyse (quantitative data)</li><li>Improves inter-rater reliability</li><li>Time-efficient and standardised – checklists and tally sheets can be used in the observation</li></ul>	<ul><li>May overlook unexpected behaviours</li><li>Limited contextual detail</li><li>Behaviours must be operationalised clearly in advance – more pre-planning is required</li></ul>
Unstructured	<ul><li>Rich, detailed data</li><li>Allows new patterns and insights to emerge</li><li>Useful in the early stages of research</li></ul>	<ul><li>Difficult to analyse and replicate</li><li>May lack consistency between observers</li><li>Higher risk of subjectivity and bias</li></ul>

Table 5.6: The strengths and limitations of structured and unstructured observations

When you are deciding whether to use a structured or unstructured observation, think about what type of data will help you answer your research question. For example:

Do I need to track and compare specific, pre-defined behaviours (for example, on-task time, aggression)?		*A structured observation with a checklist might be the most effective approach.*
Or am I more interested in exploring patterns and unexpected behaviours?		*Then an unstructured observation may be more suitable.*

Setting: Naturalistic vs controlled

Observations can be conducted in different settings, which affects the level of control the researcher has over the environment.

Naturalistic observations take place in the participant's usual environment, such as a home, school or any public space. The goal is to observe behaviour as it naturally occurs without researcher interference. Usually, naturalistic observations take an unstructured or semi-structured approach (in which a combination of field notes and codes is used).

Controlled observations take place in a structured setting, often a laboratory, where the researcher can manage variables and conditions. The goal is often to compare behaviours amongst participants.

Table 5.7 summarises the strengths and limitations of naturalistic and controlled observations.

Key concept: Bias

Observer bias occurs when an observer's expectations influence how behaviour is recorded, potentially leading to confirmation bias. Observer drift is the gradual change in how coding rules are applied over time, which can distort how data is recorded. These issues are especially important in structured observations, where consistency is crucial.

Observation type	Strengths	Limitations
Naturalistic	• High ecological validity • Behaviour is likely to be genuine • Useful for generating new hypotheses	• Limited control over extraneous variables • Hard to replicate
Controlled	• High control over variables • Easier to replicate • Can test a specific hypothesis	• Low ecological validity • Behaviour may be artificial • Risk of demand characteristics

Table 5.7: The strengths and limitations of naturalistic and controlled observations

When you are deciding whether to use a naturalistic or controlled observation, think about where you want to observe behaviour, and why. For example:

Am I aiming to capture behaviour as it naturally occurs?		*This would support a naturalistic observation.*
Or do I need more control over the environment to isolate specific behaviours?		*This would suggest a controlled observation.*

Awareness of participants: Overt vs covert

In an **overt observation**, participants are aware that they are being observed. They give informed consent in advance, making the method ethically sound. While transparency is a key advantage, the presence of an observer may influence participants' behaviour, known as reactivity.

On the other hand, **covert observations** occur where researchers do not inform the participants that they are collecting data. This is often used in a naturalistic setting, where the goal is to see authentic behaviour. Remember that if you adopt this approach, it needs to be in a public space – for example, your school playground (outdoor play area).

Table 5.8 summarises the strengths and limitations of overt and covert observations.

> **Key concept: Change**
>
> Reactivity refers to the change in behaviour that occurs when participants know they are being observed – a common issue in overt observations. This change is not due to natural development but results from the observer's presence, making the behaviour less authentic.

Observation type	Strengths	Limitations
Overt	• Ethically transparent (informed consent) • Allows open note-taking or recording • Participants have the right to withdraw	• Participants may change behaviour (reactivity) • Risk of reactivity • Lower ecological validity
Covert	• More natural behaviour (high validity) • Reduces reactivity and demand characteristics • Useful in hard-to-access environments	• Ethical concerns (lack of consent) • Limited to public or low-risk settings • Difficult to debrief participants (explain the true purpose afterwards)

Table 5.8: The strengths and limitations of overt and covert observations

When you are deciding whether to use an overt or covert observation, think about whether participants need to be aware that they are being observed. For example:

Can I ethically and practically inform participants of the observation?		*This would make it an overt observation (informed consent required).*
Would awareness change their behaviour, and am I observing in a public, low-risk space?		*A covert observation might reduce reactivity, but I would need to consider ethical implications.*

Role of the researcher: Participant vs non-participant

In **participant observation**, the researcher actively joins the group or environment being studied. By becoming involved in the participants' activities, the researcher can gain first-hand insight into behaviours, interactions and social dynamics that may not be visible from the outside. This is often viewed as one of the most credible ways in which to gain insight into participant behaviour.

However, taking notes during the observation can be challenging, as the researcher is often engaged in the activity and may not be able to record observations in real time.

This can lead to reliance on memory, which may reduce the accuracy and detail of the data. For example, a teacher conducting research in their own IB classroom.

In **non-participant observation**, the researcher remains separate from the group and does not engage in the activity being studied. This method is commonly used in structured observations, in which objectivity and minimal interference are priorities. For example, a researcher comes in to observe an IB classroom.

Table 5.9 summarises the strengths and limitations of participant and non-participant observations.

Observation type	Strengths	Limitations
Participant	<ul><li>Unique insight into behaviours and social dynamics</li><li>Access to private or sensitive behaviours</li><li>Greater understanding of context</li></ul>	<ul><li>Risk of researcher bias and loss of objectivity</li><li>Emotional involvement may affect interpretation</li><li>Note-taking is difficult during participation</li></ul>
Non-participant	<ul><li>Easier to remain objective and detached</li><li>Practical for structured or checklist-based data</li><li>Reduces researcher influence on participants</li></ul>	<ul><li>May miss subtle or contextual details</li><li>Feels distant; limited insight into participant experience</li><li>Restricted access to some settings</li></ul>

Table 5.9: The strengths and limitations of participant and non-participant observations

When you are deciding whether to use a participant or non-participant observation, think about what role you should take as an observer. For example:

Will I get a better understanding by being part of the group or activity (for example, joining a game or discussion)? *Consider a participant observation.*

Or is it more appropriate to remain outside the activity to avoid influencing it? *Then a non-participant role would help maintain objectivity.*

Example

Ainsworth's Strange Situation (1978)

Ainsworth's Strange Situation (1978) aimed to assess attachment styles in infants aged 12–18 months through eight short episodes in which the child experienced separations and reunions with their caregiver, in the presence of a stranger. Researchers observed behaviours such as proximity-seeking, exploration, separation anxiety and reunion behaviour. Based on these responses, Ainsworth identified three main attachment styles: secure, insecure-avoidant and insecure-resistant.

The study demonstrated that the quality of attachment depends on the caregiver's responsiveness and highlighted the importance of early caregiver–infant interactions in emotional and social development.

This classic study shows how design decisions are closely aligned with the researcher's aim – to investigate patterns of attachment between infants and their caregivers, demonstrating how specific choices in observational research can effectively support the research objectives (**Table 5.10**).

Factor	Design choice	Explanation
Structure	Structured	Ainsworth used a standardised sequence of episodes (for example, separations and reunions) to systematically observe specific behaviours such as proximity-seeking, exploration and distress.
Setting	Controlled	The observation took place in a lab-like environment, ensuring that each infant–caregiver pair experienced the same conditions, improving reliability.
Participant awareness	Overt	Caregivers were aware they were being observed, which may have introduced reactivity. Infants were aged 12–18 months, so they were unaware that they were being observed due to the use of a one-way mirror.
Role of researcher	Non-participant	Researchers observed from behind a one-way mirror to maintain objectivity and reduce their influence on the behaviour of participants.

Table 5.10: *Design decisions in Ainsworth's (1978) Strange Situation procedure*

Ainsworth, M. D. S., Blehar, M. C., Waters, E. and Wall, S. (1978). *Patterns of attachment: A psychological study of the strange situation.* Hillsdale, NJ: Lawrence Erlbaum.

Activity 1: Identify the observation type

For each of the following scenarios, identify the type(s) of observation being used.

You should consider all four categories:

- Structure – structured or unstructured
- Awareness – overt or covert
- Setting – naturalistic or controlled
- Researcher role – participant or non-participant

1. A researcher, with permission from the school and parents, observes toddlers during drop-off time at an early childhood setting. They tick off and record signs of attachment: crying, clinging or calm separation as the caregivers leave.

2. A psychology student sits anonymously in a café near a group of teenagers after school. Without their knowledge, the student takes field notes on how they interact, looking for signs of independence, peer conformity and emotional expression.

3. A developmental psychologist joins an early childhood setting as a volunteer to observe five-year-olds engaged in play. While participating in play, the psychologist makes mental notes about behaviours that reflect theory of mind, such as turn-taking, role-play or predicting another child's actions.

4. A developmental psychologist watches five-year-olds playing in a pretend kitchen through a two-way mirror. They tally how often children show awareness of others' thoughts and beliefs (categories such as taking on roles, predicting others' actions).

5.3 Analysing observational data

All of you need to know how to analyse observations, to learn core analysis skills. However, **only HL students** will be assessed on data analysis and interpretation (in Paper 3).

If your observation is structured, your data will require quantitative analysis. In section 2.2, you learned how to analyse quantitative data using descriptive statistics, and how to visualise the data and inferential statistics.

Activity 2: Identify the correct graph

Here are four structured observation scenarios. For each one, consider the type of data collected and decide which type of graph would be most appropriate to represent that data clearly. This could be a bar graph, histogram, box and whisker plot, line graph or scatterplot.

Scenarios

1. An observation on how often students engage in different types of play (for example, cooperative, parallel, solitary) during recess.

2. A researcher records how long each student stays on task during a 20-minute silent reading session.

3. An observer tracks the number of questions asked and the total time spent on task by each student during a science lab activity.

4. A student records how often each of five behaviours occurs during a group project: contributing ideas, staying silent, off-task behaviour, asking questions and helping peers.

An unstructured observation produces qualitative data. Researchers take the field notes and analyse the data through thematic analysis, which you learned about in section 4.5.

HL Credibility, bias, transferability

Here, you will consider qualitative data only.

Credibility

There are several ways in which you can increase credibility in observations, including:

- **Spend time in the setting (prolonged engagement)**: The longer you observe, the more familiar you become with the environment, which reduces misunderstandings and helps participants act more naturally.

- **Use triangulation**: Combine different methods (for example, observations and interviews), and use more than one researcher to critically examine your interpretation and determine whether it aligns.

- **Member checking**: Discuss your interpretations with participants (in overt studies) to confirm whether your understanding of their behaviour is accurate. Asking other researchers to review your interpretation also increases credibility.

- **Write detailed, 'thick' descriptions**: Include rich detail about the setting, people and behaviours so others can understand the full context and judge the trustworthiness.

Reducing researcher bias

There are a number of ways to prevent your own opinions from influencing the data:

- **Reflexivity**: Keep a record of your own beliefs and possible biases, and think about how they might affect your interpretation. A reflexive diary is especially important in participant observation, to reflect on the distinction between participant and researcher.

- **Use more than one observer**: When multiple observers record similar results, it shows that the data is more reliable and not just one person's opinion. An observer could be blind to the research hypothesis or question and observe the behaviour independently, then compare their recordings with those of the main researcher. The use of more than one researcher is especially important during data analysis to improve inter-rater reliability. A high level of agreement between raters increases confidence in the consistency and objectivity of the data collected.

Transferability

To ensure transferability (whether findings apply in other contexts), it is essential that you reflect on your practical and report your findings transparently. You should consider the following.

- **Give full details of the study context**: Describe where, when and with whom the study took place so others can decide if the results apply elsewhere.

- **Use a varied sample when possible**: Include participants from different backgrounds or settings to increase how broadly the findings can be applied.

- **Choose meaningful settings (theoretical sampling)**: Select participants or situations that best help you answer your research question, not just what's easiest. Naturalistic observations often have greater transferability.

- **Be honest about limitations**: Acknowledge what your study can and cannot show so others can interpret the results realistically.

Activity 3: Considering transferability

Read through the details of a particular study and then answer the reflection question

Topic: Development of self-regulation during free play

Setting: Outdoor play area at a suburban early childhood centre in a large city

Sample: 10 children (ages 4–5 years), mixed gender, observed during two 30-minute free play sessions over one week

Method: Unstructured, non-participant, overt observation. The researcher sat nearby and recorded detailed field notes on how children managed emotions, negotiated turn-taking and handled frustration.

Reflection

To what extent are the findings of this study transferable to other populations or contexts?

5.4 Class practical planning worksheet
Observation

This worksheet supports your preparation for Paper 2 Section A Question 1.
A blank version can be downloaded from collins.co.uk/internationalresources.
Ensure you design, record and justify your class practical to use as the basis for
the exam. You can record your answers in a copy of the **Class practical recording sheet**
(refer to Chapter 1). An idea for your class practical could be observing students in your
school playground at break or lunchtime.

Aim and research question

What is the aim of your investigation?	
What is the specific issue or problem you are exploring? Have you conducted background research on the behaviour?	*Consider why your practical is an important area to study, and which aspects of human development you are going to observe (for example, social interaction, peer influence, conflict resolution, gender differences).*
Why is this worth exploring in your school or community context?	

Research methodology

What type(s) of observation will you use? (For example, structured vs unstructured, naturalistic vs controlled, participant vs non-participant, overt vs covert.) Why?	*You should ensure that you are taking appropriate steps to be an ethical researcher when deciding on the type of observation you will use.*
What sampling method will you use? (For example, opportunity, purposive.) Why is this method appropriate for your context?	
Who is your target population? What sample size are you aiming for?	*Remember that you need a minimum of one participant.*
Which specific ethical considerations are needed for the observation?	*Consider how you will get informed consent from participants. You should also think about how you will conduct a debrief after the study.*

Data collection

What behaviours or categories will you observe? Will you use a coding scheme or take field notes?	*Consider which specific behaviours you will observe, as well as how you will operationalise those behaviours. If you are using codes, you should consider how you will decide upon the codes.*
Will you use event, time or point sampling to structure your observation?	
How will you record your data? (For example, tally sheets, narrative notes, video/audio with consent.)	
Which key concepts are relevant in your practical, and why?	

Data analysis

Will your analysis be quantitative, qualitative or both? Why?	
How will you analyse the quantitative and/or qualitative data?	
How will you ensure credibility, reduce bias and allow for potential transferability?	

Discussion

What are the main threats to validity or reliability?	
How could bias potentially affect the credibility of your research? How might bias influence what you choose to record?	
How could your findings be applied in real-life settings? Consider both short-term applications (immediate use in schools) and long-term applications (policy changes).	

5.5 Apply it! Paper 2 practice questions

In the previous chapters, you have practised answering Section A questions. Here, you will look at a Section B question.

Section B focuses on the evaluation of an unseen study. You will be asked to discuss two or more key concepts in relation to a study you have not seen before, which will be based on one of the four context areas (human relationships, learning and cognition, health and well-being, and human development).

This section will help you prepare. You will read an example study and model response, and then practise writing your own evaluation, applying relevant concepts to the study. Use this to develop the critical thinking and application skills you need to succeed in Paper 2 Section B.

Section B

Discuss the following study with reference to **two or more** of the following concepts: bias, change, perspective and/or responsibility.   **(15 marks)**

Example study

Three researchers conducted a covert naturalistic observation to examine group dynamics among adolescents in a public setting. Their aim was to explore how adolescents engage in leadership, inclusion/exclusion and conformity behaviours in unstructured social environments.

The researchers chose to observe teenage peer groups in a public area outside a shopping centre over a two-week period. The setting was chosen because of the high frequency of youths gathering there after school. The researchers received permission from the shopping centre to conduct the research, but did not inform the individuals being observed, in order to maintain natural behaviour. One researcher observed and took field notes while seated nearby for two hours, posing as a casual shopper. The team devised a structured coding system to identify behaviours such as who initiated decisions, how disagreement was managed, who was included or excluded from activities, and how group members responded to social pressure (for example, imitating behaviour, peer reinforcement). The frequency of these behaviours was noted by the observer.

The researchers concluded that informal group dynamics often reflect hierarchical structures and patterns of conformity, with dominant individuals influencing group decision-making. These patterns were more pronounced when groups were of the same gender.

Sample answer	Notes
This covert naturalistic observation can be discussed in terms of the concepts of responsibility, perspective and bias. It offers rich data on adolescent group dynamics, yet raises serious ethical and methodological questions.	The introduction is strong and concise. It summarises the study and signals which concepts will be discussed.
Responsibility is a key consideration in observational research, especially when it involves covert methods. Although the researchers had permission from the shopping centre, the adolescents observed were not aware they were part of a study, so the principles of informed consent and right to withdraw were breached. While observation in public spaces is sometimes acceptable, the age of participants (adolescents) introduces added responsibility to ensure they are not exposed to psychological or reputational harm. Researchers must also disseminate their findings responsibly. If these findings are presented uncritically, they could reinforce stereotypes about adolescent behaviour or lead to negative assumptions about specific age or gender groups.	The first focus is on responsibility. with links made to the study and the implications for the research.

Sample answer	Notes
The researchers' perspective and worldview may also shape their interpretation. For example, the coding category 'dominance' reflects a hierarchical lens. In some cultural or social contexts, frequent activity initiation could simply reflect enthusiasm rather than power. The study does not mention any process of reflexivity, such as how researchers considered their own assumptions about adolescent behaviour during data collection and interpretation. Reflexive field notes and member checking could have verified whether these themes truly matched the participants' intentions.	A second concept is discussed, critically examining how and why the researcher's perspective may influence the research.
Bias was considered in the design by using a structured coding system that reduced subjective judgement. However, as one researcher undertook the observation, observer bias and observer drift remain risks. Inter-coder reliability, where a second researcher codes the same footage and calculates Cohen's κ, would quantify agreement and limit subjectivity. The decision to observe covertly reduces reactivity bias and strengthens the ecological validity. However, observing in one location reduces the generalisability. The researchers could have triangulated data from multiple shopping centres, or conducted brief follow-up interviews with the adolescents, to improve credibility.	The third paragraph discusses bias, with accurate use of psychology terminology throughout.
In conclusion, while the study provides insight into adolescent group dynamics, it is ethically fragile and vulnerable to researcher bias. Addressing informed consent, incorporating reflective practice and implementing inter-coder checks would improve its ethical validity, as well as enhance its methodological credibility, across the three key concepts discussed.	A reasoned and clearly stated conclusion is given at the end.

Now you try it

Section B

Discuss the following study with reference to **two or more** of the following concepts: bias, causality, measurement and/or responsibility. **(15 marks)**

Study

Two researchers aimed to investigate whether retrieval practice (testing from memory) improves long-term memory retention more than re-reading in high school students.

A true experiment was used with an opportunity sample of 60 IB students from the same high school who were randomly assigned to two groups. Both groups were given 10 minutes to read a 600-word article on the history of space exploration.

- Group A (retrieval practice group) were given 10 minutes to write down everything they could remember from the article without using notes.

- Group B (re-reading group) were given 10 minutes to re-read the article repeatedly.

One week later, both groups returned to complete a 10-question factual recall test (the dependent variable). The researchers found that Group A scored significantly higher on average (mean = 8.2) than Group B (mean = 5.7). The result was statistically significant, demonstrating that retrieval practice led to better long-term retention.

The researchers concluded that testing can enhance memory through active retrieval. They recommended that teachers and students incorporate regular low-stakes quizzes to improve learning outcomes.

HL 5.6 Apply it! HL focus

Paper 3 Question 4 asks you to assess a claim, which is stated as the question. You are required to draw on **at least three sources** from Sources 2–5, which are provided in a Resource Booklet in the exam. You will also need to use your HL extension knowledge to provide further explanations of the points you make around the claim. The claim will always be linked to technology, motivation or culture.

In this section, you will see a model answer to help you understand how to structure a high-quality response. Then you will have the opportunity to practice writing your own answer using sample sources 2–5. Remember to ask your teacher for feedback!

The research claim is: *Screen time before going to sleep can negatively affect adolescents' academic performance.*

Remember to look back at Chapter 3.7 to see **Source 2** and Chapter 4.8 to see **Source 3**. You will need to refer to **at least one** of these sources in your answer.

Source 4

Researchers surveyed 326 adolescents aged 13–17 years from three urban schools. Participants self-reported their average screen time (spent on both smartphones and laptops) after 9:30 p.m. and provided their most recent Grade Point Average (GPA). **Table 1** shows the results.

The correlation coefficient was Pearson's $r = -0.41$, $p < 0.01$.

Table 1

Screen time before bed	Mean GPA	Sample size
< 30 minutes	3.4	104
30–90 minutes	3.0	112
> 90 minutes	2.6	111

Source 5

A study tracked 120 IB students' screen time on their phones from 9:00 p.m. to 1:00 a.m. over 12 months using an app. Academic grades were collected each term. Students with high screen use (average 100+ min/night) showed only a modest increase in academic grades across the year, from 65 per cent in Term 1 to 70 per cent in Term 4. In contrast, the low-use group demonstrated steeper progression, improving from 67 per cent to 86 per cent over the same period (average < 30 min/night). **Figure 2** shows a graph of the results.

The study indicated that screen use could have a negative impact on student learning. Findings were used to educate the community on effective sleep habits.

Figure 2

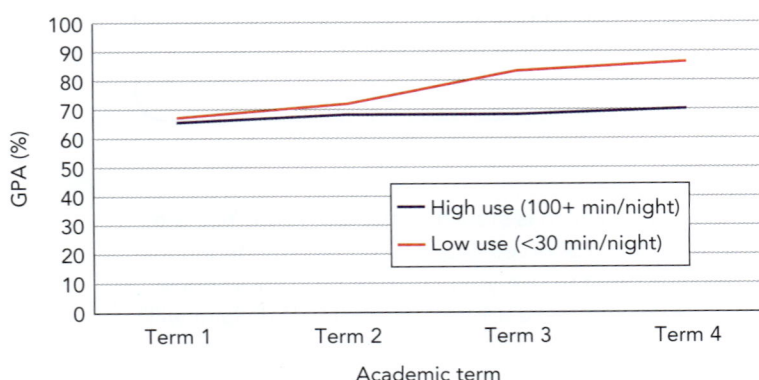

A graph showing the change in academic grades across four terms in high vs low evening screen use.

4. To what extent can we conclude that screen time before going to bed can negatively affect adolescents' academic performance? In your answer, use your own knowledge and **at least three** of Sources 2–5. **(15 marks)**

Sample answer	Notes
The claim that screen time before going to sleep can negatively affect adolescents' academic performance is supported by diverse evidence from experimental, qualitative and correlational sources. Large effect sizes in two of the quantitative studies strengthen this conclusion. However, the extent to which this relationship is causal is questioned, as there are several methodological limitations.	The introduction demonstrates a clear understanding of the claim, and issues with validity are highlighted.
Firstly, there are significant issues with construct validity. 'Screen time' is inconsistently defined in the literature – some studies measure total hours of use, others focus on specific devices such as smartphones, and few distinguish between content types or purposes (for example, recreational vs academic use). This inconsistency makes it difficult to determine what aspect of screen use is influencing academic outcomes. Additionally, both screen time and academic performance are often measured through self-reported data, which introduces social desirability bias, as students may not want to admit their screen time to researchers, which weakens the validity of study findings.	The first two paragraphs show detailed knowledge and understanding of the claim, with two types of validity issues across the sources discussed.
Another issue is the overgeneralisation of adolescence as a single developmental stage. Adolescents range from approximately 10 to 19 years old, encompassing vast differences in cognitive, emotional and academic maturity. Many studies fail to account for age-specific factors such as developmental stage, academic demands and how screen time may change during these stages, leading to oversimplified conclusions and questionable population validity.	

Sample answer	Notes
Experimental evidence (Source 2 p < 0.001) shows that students who used screens for 45 minutes before bed performed significantly worse on a reading comprehension test the following morning compared to those who read printed material (median = 5 vs median = 8). The controlled setting and physiological sleep measures strengthen internal validity. Nonetheless, comprehension scores from a single test may not fully represent academic performance, limiting ecological validity, as academic performance is typically cumulative.	
Sources 4 and 5 employ GPA as the dependent variable, a recognised standardised measure which increases reliability. Source 4 reports r = −0.41 and r² = 0.17, indicating that late-night screen use explains 17 per cent of GPA variance. However, GPA may lack cross-cultural validity as not all schools use this metric. Source 5 used a longitudinal app-tracking design, which increases ecological validity and allows for some inference of causal influence, suggesting an adverse effect of screen use on academic grades. The high screen-use group showed only a 5 per cent improvement, compared to a 19 per cent increase in the low-use group. However, the study cannot control for how participants were using their screens (for example, for homework vs. gaming), which limits the strength of the conclusions.	Different points of view are presented regarding the claim, with four sources synthesised. Each source is analysed in terms of how it supports the claim, and relevant inferences regarding validity are made.
Source 3 provides qualitative support through thematic analysis of focus group interviews. Students reported that pre-sleep screen use — often described as 'doom scrolling' — disrupted sleep routines and was perceived to hinder academic focus. While this provides real-world context, the small sample size and lack of detail regarding the questions asked or the number of responses per theme limit its credibility. Therefore, the transferability of findings is limited in studies which rely on small or context-specific samples. For instance, Source 3 interviewed only 12 students from a single school, which limits transferability. Socioeconomic and educational differences, which can significantly shape both screen habits and academic outcomes, are rarely addressed.	
Finally, there appears to be a lack of counterevidence in the sources reviewed, suggesting possible publication and confirmation biases. Potential benefits of screen use, such as improved communication, reduced cognitive load or even stress reduction, are underrepresented.	Relevant knowledge of both research methods and the HL extensions is applied.
Overall, the four sources — experimental, longitudinal, survey and qualitative — provide some support for the claim that screen time before bed is linked to poorer academic performance among adolescents. The large sample sizes used (Sources 4 and 5) further enhance the generalisability of their findings, making the claims more applicable to a wider population. While causality is difficult to determine due to methodological shortcomings, the evidence justifies cautious recommendations for limiting pre-sleep screen exposure. Further research should aim to consider a more balanced understanding of screen use, acknowledging both its risks and its potential benefits.	The conclusion is consistent with the arguments and reasoning provided in the response.

Now you try it

The research claim is: *Health and well-being mobile apps can improve student well-being.*

Remember to look back at section 3.7 to see **Source 2** and section 4.8 to see **Source 3**. You will need to refer to **at least one** of these sources in your answer.

Source 4

A study was conducted to analyse the relationship between well-being and the frequency of using mental health and well-being apps. A total of 356 upper-secondary school students who regularly used at least one well-being or mental health app (such as fitness, mindfulness or sleep apps) took part in the study. They completed a well-being questionnaire composed of two validated tools: the WHO-Five Well-Being Index, which assessed positive mood, energy levels and sleep quality, and the Perceived Stress Scale (PSS), which measured perceived stress. Participants also reported how many times per week they typically used well-being-related apps. The results are shown in **Table 2**.

Table 2

Well-being measure	Correlation coefficient
Positive mood	0.38
Energy level	0.27
Sleep quality	0.30
Stress	−0.33

A positive overall correlation was found between frequency of app use and total well-being scores: Pearson's $r = 0.35$, $p < 0.01$. Students who reported using well-being apps three or more times per week had significantly higher average well-being scores than those who used them once per week or not at all.

Source 5

A sample of 60 secondary school students took part in a study exploring the relationship between digital well-being app usage and overall well-being. All participants had used at least one type of well-being app – such as mindfulness, sleep or journalling apps – within the past six months. Each student reported their average weekly time spent using these apps (in minutes) and completed the WHO-Five Well-Being Index, a brief five-item questionnaire measuring subjective well-being, with total scores converted to a percentage from 0 to 100.

A scatterplot (**Figure 2**) showed a strong positive correlation between app use and well-being scores ($r = 0.86$, $p < 0.01$). Students who used apps for 120+ minutes per week reported higher well-being than those with minimal usage.

Figure 2

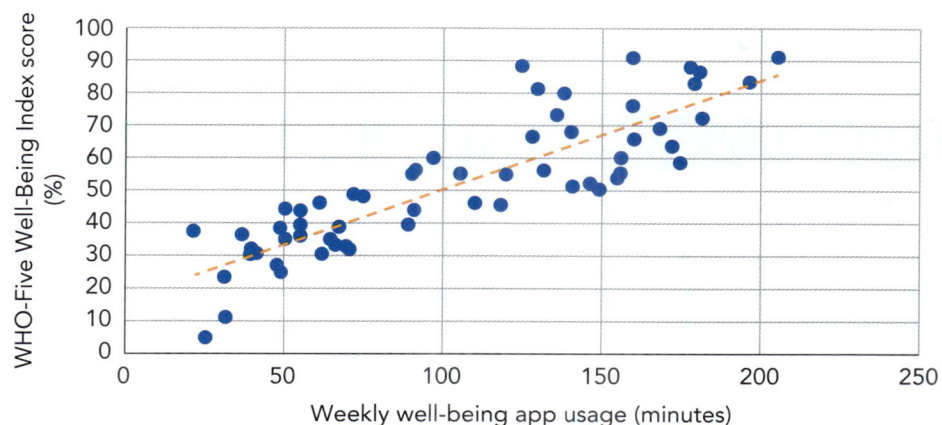

A graph to show the relationship between weekly well-being app usage and WHO-Five Well-Being scores in secondary school students.

4. To what extent can we conclude that health and well-being mobile applications can improve student well-being? In your answer, use your own knowledge and **at least three** of **Sources 2–5**. **(15 marks)**

6 Getting started with the IA research proposal

For your internal assessment (IA), you will write a 2200-word research proposal within the field of psychology. Your references and appendix will not count towards the word count, but should be included at the end of the proposal.

If you are an SL student, the IA forms 30% of your final assessment; if you are an HL student, it forms 20%.

Concept	Application
Change	You will investigate how research can bring about change. You should consider how findings may impact policy, practice or future research.
Measurement	You will need to consider how measuring behaviour requires clear **operationalisation** and valid tools.
Perspective	The research questions and tools you will choose will reflect existing psychological perspectives.
Bias	Bias may arise from personal background, sampling, participant expectations or researcher influence. You must reflect on your own position and address potential biases in both the design and interpretation of your research proposal.
Causality	You will need to consider how your chosen methodology addresses predictions, correlations or causal claims.
Responsibility	You need to ensure your proposal is designed ethically and that the research would bring a benefit to the **population of interest**.

Table 6.1: The six key concepts and their application to the IA

The research proposal

A research proposal is a document that outlines a planned research project, in which you state what, why and how you would carry out your research. In psychology, this is a vital stage in the research process for organising ideas, and gaining ethical approval and funding.

For your research proposal, you will design a study using one of the methods you used in your class practicals: survey/questionnaire, experiment (true or quasi), interview (structured, semi-structured, focus group) or observation (naturalistic or controlled, overt or covert, participant or non-participant). You will not conduct the research. Instead, the IA is based on your explanation and justification of your research decisions. You will include references and an example of your data collection tool in the appendix (these are not part of the word count).

Structure of the research proposal

Your cover or title page will include the following.

- Title of the investigation
- IB student code (an alphanumeric – for example, xyz123)
- Date, month and year of submission
- Number of words

You will then set out your research proposal using the following sections, which will be marked out of 24 marks.

- Introduction (6 marks)
- Research methodology (6 marks)
- Data collection (6 marks)
- Discussion (6 marks)
- References
- Appendix

References

When referring to ideas, theories or concepts that are not your own, you need to add a reference, both in the text and at the end of your proposal. Your references should follow IB referencing guidelines. For IB Psychology students, this is the APA (7th edition) style guide.

In the text:

- Cite the original source, using the author's name and date of publication – for example, (Perham and Vizard, 2011).
- If you use a direct quote, include the page number as well.
- If there are more than three authors, use 'et al.' after the first author's name.

When you create your reference list at the end of your research proposal, use the following example to meet requirements and maintain a consistent style.

Article title is **not** italicised; journal and volume number are.

Perham, N. and Vizard, J. (2011). Can preference for background music mediate the irrelevant sound effect? *Applied Cognitive Psychology*, *25*(4), 625–631. **DOI or retrieved from URL**

Only include if the article is online (the DOI is preferred).

All words in journal title should be capitalised.

Appendix

Use the appendix to present your data collection tool (refer to section 6.3). Give your appendix a heading – for example, **Appendix A: [Title of tool used]**.

Getting started

Before you begin your research proposal, you need to make some important decisions.

1. What is the population you are interested in studying?

You need to identify the population of interest (target population), which is a group of people who share something in common (such as experiences, characteristics). As you are not carrying out the research, you can select the **sample** from a school, local or national community.

> **Key concept: Responsibility**
>
> It is important that you follow the principles of academic integrity when writing your IA. Your written research proposal should be authentically your own work. Where you refer to existing studies or theories, you should cite and reference them. Artificial intelligence (AI) is a tool that can assist research; you should never use it to write your proposal. You should reference any AI prompt.

2. What psychological problem will you explore?

The problem needs to be relevant to the target population you have chosen. You could start by considering which topics you have found most interesting or whether there is a real-world problem that would benefit from psychological research.

3. Is it ethically and practically viable?

In practical terms, you must be able to study your research proposal using one of the methods covered in your class practicals. Remember, however, that you will not conduct the research.

You are responsible for following the ethical considerations of informed consent, protection from stress/harm, anonymity and confidentiality, right to withdraw, unjustified deception and debriefing. The IB does not allow studies that could cause harm, such as ingestion or animal research. Ask your teacher for a full list of exclusions.

4. What is your research question?

At this point, you will be ready to create your research question. Here is an example of a research question:

What is the effect of background music (with lyrics vs without lyrics) on high school students' working memory while studying?

Notice that the question is focused on a target population (high school students), there is a real-world problem (effective study habits) and a method is suggested that could be used (experiment).

Once you have made all these decisions, submit a plan of your IA research proposal to your teacher. Use the *IA research proposal planning worksheet* in section 6.5 to help you.

Reflection activity

Which topics have you enjoyed so far in the IB DP Psychology course? Are there any areas you want to explore further? How could these be used to develop a study?

6.1 Understanding criterion A: Introduction

In the introduction, you must justify why your research is needed. You must indicate any previous research and the significance of your proposed study. The mark scheme identifies three key aspects – aim, description and research – which together are worth 6 marks.

Aim of the research

Write your aim at the end of the introduction. It should be short, focused and state what you intend to study. Make sure that it links to both the real-life problem and the population of interest. You could use this structure: *The aim of this proposal is to investigate [psychological concept] in [target population] in relation to [real-life problem].*

Command terms: Criterion A: Justify

The command term 'justify' means to provide support and evidence for why your problem is worth investigating with the population of interest.

Description of the real-life problem

Begin by explaining the psychological problem you are focusing on. This should be an area you are genuinely curious about. It should also be a real issue affecting people in society today – for example:

- Sleep and mental health
- Body image and self-esteem
- Stress and memory

Explain what the problem is and why it matters. For example: *Sleep deprivation is a condition in which individuals consistently get insufficient or poor-quality sleep. This is a problem because…*

You must clearly define the population of interest – the larger group of people who are affected by the psychological problem you are exploring. This is different from the sample (**Figure 6.1**). The sample refers to the specific individuals who would participate in the study, to allow you to make inferences about your population of interest.

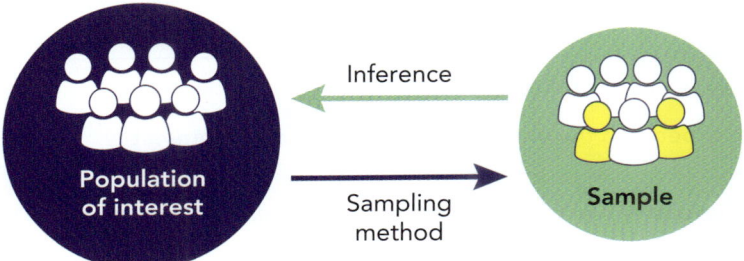

Figure 6.1: The relationship between the population of interest and sample

To help you identify the population of interest, ask yourself:

- Who is most affected by this issue in real life?
- What characteristics or contextual factors (such as age) relate to this group?

For example: *This issue is particularly relevant to high school students aged 15–18 years, who often report insufficient sleep and high levels of academic stress.*

Link to relevant research

It is important to do some wider background research and reading around your topic area. From this, select two pieces of research to include in your research proposal – you want to summarise the findings and conclusions from each. The procedural details are not important unless they are directly relevant to your proposal (that is, you intend to use a similar tool).

Use these questions to help you identify the relevant information:

- What did each study find? What were the main conclusions?
- How does each study relate to the psychological problem I'm investigating?
- Do the studies help explain why this issue matters for my population of interest?
- Do the findings support or challenge the assumptions of my chosen original study?
- How do the studies help justify the need for my investigation?

Mark scheme: Introduction

Your introduction, worth 6 marks, will be assessed using the following mark scheme.

Mark	Level descriptor
0	The work does not reach a standard described by the descriptors below.
1–2	• The aim or research question is stated but not clearly expressed or is too broad. • The real-life problem is stated. • The findings and conclusions of two pieces of research are not clearly stated and are not made relevant to the investigation, or only one piece of research is included.
3–4	• The aim or research question is clearly stated but only partially focused. • The real-life problem is described, but the impact on the population of interest is not addressed. • Relevant findings and conclusions of two pieces of research are described and linked to the investigation or only one is explained and linked to the investigation.
5–6	• The aim or research question is clearly stated and focused. • The real-life problem is described and the impact on the population of interest is explained. • Relevant findings and conclusions of two pieces of research are explained and linked to the investigation.

Example

Research question: 'What is the effect of background music (with lyrics vs without lyrics) on serial recall in high school students?'

Sample text	Assessment criteria
A common challenge faced by high school students is identifying and applying effective study strategies. In academic environments, students face heavy workloads. Therefore, they often rely on easier strategies, which can give the illusion of learning. For example, students frequently use low-utility strategies such as re-reading, highlighting and cramming, rather than higher-utility techniques such as retrieval practice and spaced repetition (Dunlosky et al., 2013).	The real-life problem is described: *students often use ineffective study habits.*
While many students are highly motivated, they often rely on methods that feel intuitively helpful but are not necessarily supported by cognitive science research. This disconnect between perception and evidence findings suggests that many students are unaware of how to study in a way that supports effective learning. Ineffective study strategies can be a barrier to academic performance, which can increase stress and lower self-esteem, ultimately negatively affecting an individual´s well-being over time. This makes it essential to investigate how study environments and habits influence learning and memory. One widely adopted study habit is listening to music	The impact on the population of interest is explained: *decreased working memory function on high school students.*

Sample text	Assessment criteria
while studying, as it is believed to improve focus and motivation. However, when students engage in learning activities that require them to hold and manipulate verbal information, background music with lyrics may interfere with the functioning of working memory.	
Salamé and Baddeley (1982) investigated how unattended background speech affects short-term memory, focusing on immediate serial recall of visually presented verbal material. Their research provided foundational evidence for the irrelevant sound effect – the phenomenon in which irrelevant auditory input disrupts memory performance, even when it is not consciously attended to. In a series of experiments, participants were asked to recall sequences of letters while exposed to irrelevant speech, such as digits or nonsense syllables. Performance was significantly worse under these conditions compared to silence or white noise. Crucially, the interference occurred even when participants were instructed to ignore the background speech, suggesting that the effect is automatic and involuntary. Their findings were explained using the working memory model (Baddeley and Hitch, 1974), specifically the phonological loop, which is responsible for processing verbal and auditory input. When individuals attempt to rehearse verbal material, background speech competes for the same cognitive resources, overloading the phonological loop and impairing working memory performance.	Research 1 is explained.
Building on this, Perham and Vizard (2011) explored the effects of different types of background music on serial recall. They compared conditions involving silence, instrumental music and music with lyrics, while also examining whether personal music preference moderated the effect. Their results showed that music with lyrics significantly impaired recall, supporting the idea that verbal content disrupts verbal rehearsal. Moreover, preferred music was just as disruptive as non-preferred music, challenging the belief that enjoyment of music can mitigate its negative cognitive effects.	Research 2 is explained.
Understanding how background music influences working memory is important for helping students make informed decisions about their study habits. Both studies provide empirical evidence that listening to music with lyrics impairs recall. Therefore, students may benefit from choosing silence or instrumental music when studying. Investigating these effects can provide meaningful insights into how environmental factors impact learning outcomes. Therefore, this proposal aims to investigate the effect of background music (with and without lyrics) on high school students' performance in a recall task.	A link is made between the research and the investigation. The clear and focused aim is given.
(Word total: 523)	

6.2 Understanding criterion B: Research methodology

In the research methodology, you must justify your choice of research method and then explain your procedure. You must also explain what ethical considerations you would need to take if you were conducting the study. This section is worth 6 marks.

Justify your choice of research method

You must choose one of the research methods you used in your class practicals, such as:

- a survey/questionnaire
- an experiment (true or quasi)
- an interview (structured, semi-structured or focus group)
- an observation (naturalistic or controlled, overt or covert, participant or non-participant).

You then need to explain why your choice of research method is appropriate for your investigation. In other words, highlight the benefits of using that method.

Use these questions to help you form your justification:

- Why is this method the best fit for my research question?
- What kind of data will this method collect: quantitative or qualitative?
- Does it allow me to explore cause-and-effect relationships, attitudes or perceptions?

Explain the procedure

This is the most technical part of your research proposal. Be thorough and specific. You need to explain the sampling technique, the characteristics of the sample, the design (if you are using an experiment), the setting and the process that you would undertake. Ultimately, you are showing why your chosen research method is appropriate for your investigation.

To help you explain your procedure, ask yourself:

- How will I recruit my participants?
- Are there any specific characteristics the sample needs to have?
- What variables am I manipulating or measuring (experiment)?
- What are the exact steps I need to take, from start to finish?

> **Command terms: Criterion B: Explain**
>
> The command term 'explain' means to give a detailed account with reasoning on the planning of your research methodology.

Explain the ethical considerations

You need to show how to be a responsible researcher by explaining the ethical considerations relevant to your investigation, stating how you would deal with each one.

As you consider this, ask yourself:

- How will I ensure participants understand the study to give fully informed consent?
- What might make them uncomfortable, and how can I minimise this?
- How will I protect participants' identities and data?
- If I am using a vulnerable group or children under 16 years, what steps will I take to ensure their safety?

Mark scheme: Introduction

Your research methodology, worth 6 marks, will be assessed using the following mark scheme.

Mark	Level descriptor
0	The work does not reach a standard described by the descriptors below.
1–2	• The research method is described with errors in understanding. • The procedure is described but is unclear due to errors or omissions. • Ethical considerations are described but not linked to the investigation.
3–4	• The choice of research method is described. • The procedure is described but lacks detail. • Relevant ethical considerations are described but some are not linked to the investigation.
5–6	• The choice of research method is explained. • The procedure is explained. • Relevant ethical considerations are described and explicitly linked to the investigation.

Example

Research question: 'What is the effect of background music (with lyrics vs without lyrics) on serial recall in high school students?'

Sample text	Assessment criteria
This investigation will use a true experiment with an independent measures design to examine the effect of background music on working memory capacity. This method is appropriate because it allows for the manipulation of an independent variable (type of background noise) and the measurement of the effect on a dependent variable (working memory performance), enabling cause-and-effect conclusions to be drawn. Additionally, the controlled environment can ensure standardisation — in this case, ensuring each participant listens to the exact same type of background noise and completes the same task. An independent measures design is chosen to reduce the practice effect, whereby repeating the task could improve performance. Thus, participants will be randomly allocated to one condition. The independent variable is the type of background auditory condition, with three conditions: 1. Silence (no background sound) 2. Music with no lyrics (instrumental) 3. Music with lyrics (verbal music in English)	The choice of research method is explained.

Sample text	Assessment criteria
The dependent variable is participants' working memory performance, operationalised through a modified digit span test using letter sequences. No credit will be given for letters recalled in the wrong order.	
The sample will consist of 45 first-year IB high school students, aged 16–17 years, recruited through opportunity sampling from one international school. This will be obtained by asking three tutor groups if they would like to participate in the study. IB students are chosen as they undertake regular studying, with similar working memory demands. Therefore, they will reflect the population of interest for this investigation. The experiment will take place in three quiet classrooms during a morning registration, with standardised instructions and materials to ensure consistency between conditions.	
Each participant will be tested individually with headphones, a laptop and an answer sheet. Participants in all conditions will complete the task while listening to the background noise in their condition. Participants will be presented with a sequence of consonants, one at a time, at a rate of one letter per second via a computer screen. Immediately following the sequence, participants will be asked to write down the letters in the same order they were shown. There will be eight trials with different letter lists.	The procedure is explained.
To ensure ethical standards are upheld, permission will be gained by the IB coordinator to use registration time. All participants will be given an informed consent form outlining the purpose of the study, the anonymity of their data and their right to withdraw. The study is similar to the setup of classroom activities and therefore has minimal harm. However, consideration has been given to have the volume set below 65 decibels to reduce auditory harm. Also, the music with lyrics will be a popular song and will not include offensive language. All participants will receive a debriefing following the experiment to explain that the study was measuring the effect of music on studying. The findings will be shared during an assembly to educate the year group about study habits.	Ethical considerations are explained and explicitly liked to the investigation.
(Word total: 479)	

6.3 Understanding criterion C: Data collection

In this section, you must clearly explain how you will collect your data and why your chosen tool measures what it intends to measure. This is a way of demonstrating the construct validity of your research. This section is worth 6 marks.

Choose and describe one data collection tool

You must select **one** data collection tool that matches the behaviour or variable your study is investigating. While you can use existing tools, your tool must be created by you.

> **Command terms: Criterion C: Justify and explain**
>
> The command term 'justify and explain' means to provide support for your decisions on your data collection tool and explain those decisions.

Examples of acceptable data collection tools include the following.

- A questionnaire or Likert-scale survey
- An interview guide (for structured or semi-structured interviews)
- An observation checklist (to record specific behaviours in a setting)
- A test or task sheet (for example, a memory recall task in an experiment)

Explain the design of your data collection tool

Explain why you designed your data collection tool the way you did and the steps you took to ensure it measures your variable or construct accurately. Your tool must include a **minimum of five distinct items**. For example, for a survey/questionnaire or interview, there must be at least five questions.

Put a copy of your data collection tool in the **appendix** and refer to its location in your research proposal – for example, '(see Appendix A)'. You do not need to include any other materials, including consent forms, in your appendix. Content in the appendix is **not** included in the word count.

It is good practice to conduct a **pilot test**, a small-scale trial of your procedure, before the actual data collection. It helps identify and fix any issues, especially with the tools used for data collection. In the write up of your research proposal, mention what your pilot test was, the feedback you received and what you changed.

When you are considering your tool design and evaluating it, you want to use key terminology. The guiding questions in **Table 6.2** will help you consider steps you could take in the design of your tool.

Key term	Definition	Guiding questions
Operationalisation	Defining abstract concepts in measurable or observable terms	• How did I choose or write the items, questions or behaviours in the tool? • If I used a scale (for example, 1–5), what did the scale points represent? • Are the behaviours/categories clearly defined?
Construct validity	The extent to which the tool measures the psychological construct being studied	• Did I base my tool on an existing measurement or theory? • Does my tool reflect the theoretical definitions I found when doing wider research? • Are all aspects of the construct represented?
Reliability	The consistency of the tool over time or across researchers	• Is the procedure or tool standardised and replicable? • Do I plan to test the tool through a pilot test? • For observations: Is there a clear checklist of behaviours? • For interviews: How far is the interview guide consistent?

Key term	Definition	Guiding questions
Face validity	The degree to which the tool appears to measure what it intends to	• Would someone unfamiliar with the study agree the tool matches the aim? • Is the language appropriate for the population?
Internal validity (quantitative)	The degree the change in the dependent variable can be attributed to the independent variable	• How can I ensure the outcome is really caused by my manipulated variable? • How have I considered control of variables and standardisation in the design?
Credibility (qualitative)	The trustworthiness of the findings and the degree this matches participants' experiences	• Do I plan to use techniques such as member checking, triangulation or prolonged engagement? • Have I reflected on researcher bias (reflexivity)?

Table 6.2: Concepts and questions to consider when you are designing your data collection tool

Explain the potential challenges in data collection

You must consider what could make your results less reliable, valid or credible. This shows critical thinking and awareness of research limitations. Common challenges to consider include:

- **Participant challenges**: Participant variability, demand characteristics, social desirability, recall bias, fatigue effect
- **Methodological challenges**: Order and practice effects, confounding variables, wording of questions, ambiguous scales
- **Researcher challenges**: Interviewer effects, researcher bias

Mark scheme: Data collection

Your data collection, worth 6 marks, will be assessed using the following mark scheme.

Command terms: Criterion C: Measurement

In psychological research, measurement refers to how constructs such as stress, self-esteem or memory are translated into observable variables. In Criterion C, your proposal is assessed on the appropriateness and clarity of your measurement tool. Use operationalisation, reliability, validity and/or credibility to explicitly strengthen your justification.

Mark	Level descriptor
0	The work does not reach a standard described by the descriptors below.
1–2	• An appropriate data collection tool has been created to measure behaviour, but it contains errors. • Decisions made when **creating the data collection** tool are in limited detail or have limited relevance to the aim or research question of the investigation. • Potential challenges when **collecting data** are described in limited detail and/or are not relevant to the investigation.

Mark	Level descriptor
3–4	• An appropriate data collection tool has been created to measure behaviour. • Decisions made when creating the data collection tool are described and relevant to the aim or research question of the investigation. • Potential challenges when collecting data are described and relevant to the investigation.
5–6	• An appropriate and effective data collection tool to measure behaviour has been created. • Decisions made when creating the data collection tool are explained and relevant to the aim or research question of the investigation. • Potential challenges when collecting data are explained and relevant to the investigation.

Example

Research question: 'What is the effect of background music (with lyrics vs without lyrics) on serial recall in high school students?'

Sample text	Assessment criteria
The data collection tool used in this investigation is a modified digit span task, a widely used psychological test to measure working memory capacity. However, this investigation will use letters instead of numbers, with participants attempting to recall increasingly longer sequences of consonants (see Appendix A). This was chosen as it would give a clearer measure of working memory capacity, rather than measuring serial recall performance. Using letters instead of digits also reduces the likelihood of participants relying on familiar number patterns, which could aid recall through chunking.	An appropriate and effective tool to measure behaviour is created.
The task consists of eight trials, spanning the length from four to eight letters, presented on laptops using a pre-recorded video to ensure standardised timing. Each letter sequence appears on screen for one second, followed by the prompt RECALL for participants to write the sequence in order on a structured answer sheet.	
A random generator was used to generate the sequences with consonants only. This was to reduce researcher bias. Each sequence was then reviewed and edited to ensure that it did not include phonologically similar letters (for example, B/D, M/N), which could cause associations to be made and potentially confound the results. A practice trial will be done to familiarise participants with the task (4 letters) and ensure they understand the procedure before commencing the study. The tool will be pilot tested with a small group of students to confirm clarity of instructions and task difficulty, ensuring that the tool effectively measures verbal working memory under different auditory conditions. All trials will be administered individually on laptops with a video with automated times built in, ensuring standardisation across all conditions and reducing the potential for researcher influence.	Decisions made about the tool are explained and relevant to the aim.

Sample text	Assessment criteria
Several challenges to data collection are anticipated. First, participant variability in working memory ability between the independent groups could influence recall performance. However, as the sample is homogenous and from the same year group, this could reduce variability in responses. Additionally, while the task will not take long to complete, fatigue effect could still be present. Therefore, only 10 trials are included to reduce cognitive load, while still providing reliable data. *Demand characteristics may occur if participants guess the purpose of the study and alter their performance accordingly. To reduce this risk, participants will not be informed of the specific hypothesis and all instructions will be delivered using a standardised, neutral script. Additionally, test anxiety could influence performance for some students. Therefore, conducting the experiment individually in a quiet, familiar environment aims to minimise this effect.* *Lastly, while the task offers high internal validity due to its standardisation and objective scoring criteria, external validity may be limited. The study setting and artificial task may not fully represent real-life memory use and the types of information students usually manipulate when studying. Nonetheless, the tool remains well-suited for testing the specific cognitive process under investigation.* (Word total: 469)	Potential challenges when collecting data are explained and relevant to the aim.

Appendix A: Modified digit span task

Instructions to participants: *You will see a list of letters appear one at a time. Try to remember them in the exact order. After the final letter, the word 'RECALL' will appear. Write down the letters you remember in the order they were shown.*

Practice trial (4 letters): F – K – J – M

Test trials (4 letters to 11 letters):

4 letters	T – V – G – P
5 letters	B – C – L – Y – H
6 letters	M – R – D – S – K – X
7 letters	W – Z – T – J – Q – N – L
8 letters	S – H – F – V – Y – B – K – D
9 letters	L – G – C – M – W – P – X – H – R
10 letters	Y – J – N – Z – B – R – D – T – L – V
11 letters	C – M – K – H – Q – S – G – W – T – F – P

Scoring criteria: Participants receive a span score equal to the longest sequence they recall correctly, with all of the letters remembered in the correct order. Maximum score = 11.

> **Activity 1: Choosing a data collection tool**
>
> For the following research proposals, identify the most appropriate data collection tool. Explain why this tool is suitable and mention at least one challenge that could arise with the tool.
>
> **Scenario 1: Survey**
>
> *'A student is researching whether there is a relationship between social media use and self-esteem among teenagers.'*
>
> **Scenario 2: Interview**
>
> *'A student wants to explore how first-generation university students experience academic pressure and motivation.'*
>
> **Scenario 3: Observation**
>
> *'A student is studying the impact of peer presence on helping behaviour in a public setting.'*

6.4 Understanding criterion D: Discussion

The final section is the discussion, in which you show that your investigation has application beyond the experiment itself. It is important to reflect on how your research could impact others, what limitations may influence your findings and how future research could explore the topic further. This section is worth 6 marks.

Potential findings and implications for practice and/or policy

In this section, you need to address the following points.

- Describe the results you expect based on theory and previous research.

- Explain how this would affect real life – for example, school policies, teaching strategies, other groups' behaviour beyond your population of interest. It is important to consider short-term and long-term implications.

- Use phrases like *'The findings might lead to...'* or *'This could inform...'*.

Reflection on researcher bias

You must show insight into how your own background may have influenced your study. This increases validity or credibility. Questions you might ask yourself include:

- Why did I choose this topic? Did I have personal experience of it?

- Did I have existing assumptions about the real-life problem that could have led to confirmation bias?

- Do any of my personal views or beliefs influence the research?

Explain an additional method

You must suggest **one** other method that could be used to gain new insights – this is in addition to your own research, not an alternative to it. If your research proposal gathers only one type of data, adding a different method could be a useful form of

> **Command terms:**
> **Criterion D: Discuss**
>
> The command term 'discuss' means to offer a balanced view by synthesising evidence to create a clear argument about the implications of your research and the limitations.

method triangulation. For example, when using an experiment (quantitative), adding an interview could be useful (qualitative). It is important to explain *why* this would create a more **holistic** understanding of the topic and help the population of interest. If you do not include an additional method, this section will be capped at the middle band (3–4 marks)!

Mark scheme: Discussion

Your discussion, worth 6 marks, will be assessed using the following mark scheme.

Mark	Level descriptor
0	The work does not reach a standard described by the descriptors below.
1–2	• Potential findings of the investigation are described but the implication(s) for policy/ practice are not addressed. • One or more examples of researcher bias are identified. • The usefulness of one relevant additional research method is described, without reference to increasing the understanding of the area of investigation.
3–4	• Potential findings of the investigation are described and the implication(s) for policy/ practice are partially addressed. • One or more relevant examples of researcher bias are described. • The usefulness of one relevant additional research method is discussed without reference to increasing the understanding of the area of investigation.
5–6	• Potential findings of the investigation are described in detail and the implication(s) for policy/practice are explained. • One or more relevant examples of how researcher bias may affect the investigation are discussed. • The usefulness of one relevant additional research method is discussed with reference to increasing the understanding of the area of investigation.

Example

Research question: 'What is the effect of background music (with lyrics vs without lyrics) on serial recall in high school students?'

Sample text	Assessment criteria
This investigation may lead to one of two key findings. If the null hypothesis is accepted, it would suggest that background music with lyrics does not significantly affect students' working memory capacity while studying. However, if the null hypothesis is rejected, and music with lyrics significantly impairs performance compared to instrumental music or silence, it would support the theory that verbal distractions interfere with the phonological loop in working memory due to the irrelevant sound effect.	The potential findings of the investigation are described.

Sample text	Assessment criteria
Should the null hypothesis be rejected, there would be meaningful implications for the school community. For example, sessions could be planned in the IB DP course to educate students on effective study habits, incorporating evidence-based advice on the impact of multitasking and background music on studying. Additionally, there could be teacher training and workshops held with parents on using cognitive science to understand study habits. This could ensure all stakeholders in the community have a shared understanding and language about effective study habits. If the music group (no lyrics) does better than silence, instrumental or lo-fi music could be played in study areas in the school. Universities and colleges could also apply the findings to inform study skills programmes, ensuring continuity between age groups.	The implication(s) for policy/practice are explained.
As a high school student, I recognise that personal biases may have influenced my approach to this investigation. I frequently listen to music while studying and have found it personally motivating, which may have shaped my initial assumptions about its effectiveness. Additionally, as an IB DP psychology student, prior exposure to the working memory model may have introduced confirmation bias, leading me to expect a particular outcome. My cultural background may also contribute to bias, as I come from a culture that places a strong emphasis on academic success and diligent study habits, potentially reinforcing my belief in the importance of optimising study environments.	Two examples of researcher biases are explained.
To minimise the influence of these biases, I selected an experimental method using an objective measures based on an existing psychological test, and implemented standardised procedures with randomised group allocation. The experiment was conducted using individual laptops with automated timings to ensure consistency and reduce variability in how each participant experienced the task.	
However, this study does have several limitations. Firstly, it measures only the short-term effects of background music on memory and does not allow conclusion on the long-term effects on academic performance. Additionally, individual differences in working memory capacity and existing habits in the sample were not accounted for. The use of a serial recall task, while effective for isolating verbal working memory, may limit ecological validity. Real-world studying typically involves processing and integrating more complex and meaningful information than simple letter sequences. As such, the task may not fully reflect the cognitive demands of authentic study experiences.	
To deepen our understanding of how music affects learning, future research could use a semi-structured interview method. Interviewing students about their music habits, preferences and study outcomes could offer insight into why students choose certain types of music and whether they are aware of the potential cognitive effects. It would also allow exploration of emotional or motivational reasons behind music use, which are not addressed in a quantitative study. Combining these perspectives with experimental data would produce a richer and more holistic view of how music influences academic performance.	A relevant additional research method is explained, with reference to increasing the understanding of the area of investigation.
(Word total: 543)	

6.5 IA research proposal planning worksheet

This worksheet will help you prepare for your IA. A blank version can be downloaded from collins.co.uk/internationalresources. Ensure that you consider each of the different requirements needed for your research proposal. Your teacher will approve your plan. After this, they can only provide feedback on one draft of your IA.

Introduction (6 marks)

Who have you chosen to study as your population of interest? Why?	
What real-life issue does your investigation address, and why is it important?	
What is your aim and how is it relevant to the population of interest?	
Summarise the findings and conclusions of your first relevant piece of research. Include how it relates to your aim.	
Summarise the findings and conclusions of your second relevant piece of research. Include how it relates to your aim.	

Research methodology (6 marks)

What is your chosen research method (experiment, interview, observation, survey) and why is it appropriate? Link explicitly to your aim.	
What are the key decisions you made about the procedure (sampling, design, setting, process)?	
What ethical considerations are relevant and how will you address them? Be specific to what you are studying.	

Data collection (6 marks)

What data collection tool will you use and how does it measure what you are intending to measure?	
Why did you design your tool in this way? Include choices made about questions, format and/or operationalisation.	
Include any of your initial planning of your tool here (for example, sample questions for your interview guide, your Likert scale).	
What challenges might arise in collecting your data (participant variability, bias, tool limitations)?	

Discussion (6 marks)

What are the possible findings and what might they imply for practice or policy?	
How might your own background, values or experiences influence your research (researcher bias)?	
What additional method could be used to investigate this topic and how would it increase understanding?	

IB DP Psychology IA final checklist

Use this form as a final checklist before submitting your research proposal. A blank version can be downloaded from collins.co.uk/internationalresources. Read through your research proposal carefully and tick off each item on this checklist as you find it in your work. This will help ensure you meet both the assessed and the formatting requirements for the IA.

General formatting

☐ I have included a cover or title page that includes:

  ☐ Title of the investigation

  ☐ IB student code (alphanumeric – for example, xyz123)

  ☐ Date, month and year of submission

  ☐ Number of words

☐ My report is a written document (I have only included tables and graphs where relevant).

☐ I have used Arial or Times Rew Roman font, size 12pt, double spaced.

☐ My report does not exceed 2200 words, excluding references and appendix (note that examiners will stop reading beyond this limit).

☐ My citations follow the APA 7th Edition (or my schools suggested referencing style) and I have provided a list of references at the end of my research proposal.

☐ I have included an appendix with my data collection tool.

☐ I have proofread my report for spelling and grammar mistakes. This includes ensuring the proposal is free from identifying information about the school.

Criterion A: Introduction (6 marks)

☐ My research aim is relevant and clearly focused on the population of interest.

☐ I have described a real-life problem and explained its impact on the population of interest.

☐ My topic is interesting and relevant to students.

☐ I have summarised the findings and conclusions of **at least two pieces** of psychological research.

☐ I have clearly linked the research to the aim and topic of my investigation.

Criterion B: Research methodology (6 marks)

☐ I have justified my choice of research method (experiment, interview, observation or survey).

☐ I have explained the procedure (sampling technique, sample characteristics, setting and process).

☐ I believe the method is appropriate for answering the research question.

☐ I have identified and explained ethical considerations.

☐ I have described steps to minimise or address ethical concerns.

Criterion C: Data collection (6 marks)

☐ I have selected one data collection tool (for example, questionnaire, Likert scale, checklist or interview guide).

☐ My data collection tool contains **at least five items**.

☐ I have included the tool in the appendix and referred to in the main text.

☐ I have explained the decisions I made in designing the tool (for example, operationalising variables, selecting questions).

☐ I have discussed any potential challenges in data collection (for example, bias, fatigue, validity, order effects).

Criterion D: Discussion (6 marks)

☐ I have described the potential findings of the study.

☐ I have discussed the implications for policy and/or practice.

☐ I have identified and discussed researcher bias (personal experiences, beliefs, culture, values).

☐ I have proposed **one additional method** to investigate the topic further.

☐ I have justified the additional method in terms of how it could improve understanding of the topic.

Glossary

Acquiescence bias: A type of response bias in which participants tend to agree with statements regardless of their actual beliefs.

Active listening: A communication technique that involves fully concentrating on, understanding, remembering and responding to what participants said.

Aim: A general statement describing what the researcher intends to investigate.

Bar graph: A graphical representation of data using rectangular bars to compare different categories.

Bias: A deviation from objective thinking, often resulting from an individual's prior experiences, preferences or cultural influences. Common forms include:

- **Confirmation bias:** Seeking or interpreting information in a way that confirms prior beliefs.

- **Interviewer bias:** When the interviewer's expectations, behaviour, or tone influences the responses of the participant.

- **Participant bias:** When participants act in ways they believe the researcher expects.

- **Publication bias:** A tendency to publish only significant results.

- **Researcher bias:** When the researcher unintentionally influences the outcome.

- **Sampling bias:** When the sample does not accurately reflect the population.

Box and whisker plot: A graphical representation of a data set that displays its distribution based on a five-number summary: minimum, first quartile, median, third quartile and maximum.

Causality: The idea that one variable directly influences or causes a change in another, which is known as a cause-and-effect relationship. In complex behaviour, multiple causes may interact.

Case study: An in-depth exploration of a single case, which could be a person, group or situation. Often uses multiple methods and provides rich qualitative data.

Change: A key concept describing how variables alter over time – for example, developmental change measured in longitudinal studies.

Closed-ended question: A question that provides fixed response options such as 'yes' or 'no'. Useful in structured interviews and surveys/questionnaires.

Coding : The process of systematically organising and categorising qualitative data into meaningful themes or patterns to allow for analysis and interpretation.

Collectivism: A cultural orientation that emphasises group goals, social harmony, and interdependence over personal autonomy. It is often contrasted with individualism, which values independence and self-expression.

Confounding variable: An external variable that may affect the dependent variable and interfere with the results of an experiment, reducing internal validity.

Construct validity: Is the tool a truthful measure of the psychological concept?

Controlled observation: An observation carried out under controlled conditions, often in a lab.

Controlled variable: A factor that is kept constant across all conditions of an experiment to ensure a fair test.

Correlation coefficient: A numerical index (usually between −1 and +1) representing the strength and direction of a relationship between two variables.

Correlational study: Non-experimental research method that examines the relationship between two or more variables without manipulating them.

Counterbalancing: A procedure used in a repeated measures design to control for order effects by varying the sequence of conditions among participants – for example, half do A→B and the other half B→A.

Covert observation: A research method in which participants are unaware they are being observed, allowing for natural behaviour without influence from the observer's presence.

Credibility: How believable and trustworthy a study's findings are. Particularly relevant in qualitative research and can be enhanced through techniques like member checking and triangulation.

Cross-sectional: Research that involves looking at data from a population at one specific point in time.

Deductive approach: A top-down research approach that begins with a theory or hypothesis, then gathers data to test it.

Demand characteristics: When participants are able to guess the aim of the study and alter their behaviour accordingly.

Dependent variable: The variable that is measured in an experiment; it is expected to change due to manipulation of the independent variable.

Descriptive statistics: Statistical techniques that allow researchers to summarise and describe the main features of a dataset without making inferences about causality.

Dominant responder bias: Occurs when one (or a few) participants in a group setting dominates the discussion, potentially influencing the responses of others.

Double-blind design: A method in experimental research in which neither the participants nor the experimenters knows who is receiving the treatment or the placebo, preventing bias.

Ecological validity: The extent to which the findings of a study can be generalised to real-life settings. Higher ecological validity means the research context closely resembles real-world conditions.

Enculturation: The process by which individuals learn and adopt the values, norms, customs and behaviours of their culture, typically through observation and instruction.

Ethical considerations: The principles and guidelines researchers must follow to protect the well-being and rights of participants. These include informed consent, confidentiality, the right to withdraw, protection from harm and debriefing.

Experimental design: The way in which participants are allocated to groups in an experiment.

Extraneous variables: Any variables not being investigated in a study which have the potential to influence the dependent variable.

Face validity: Whether a test appears, on the surface, to measure what it claims to measure. It is the weakest and most subjective form of validity.

Fatigue effect: A type of order effect in which participants become tired or bored over time, which can reduce the reliability of their performance in repeated tasks.

Field notes: Detailed notes taken by researchers during or after observations, recording behaviours, contexts and personal reflections.

Focus group: A group interview technique that collects data through group interaction on a topic determined by the researcher; often used in qualitative research.

Frequency table: A chart that shows how frequently each value in a set of data occurs.

Generalisability: The degree to which the findings or conclusions of a study can be applied to other populations or settings, reflecting the research's external validity.

Graph (chart): A visual tool used to represent data, commonly employed in psychology to display patterns, trends or relationships between variables. Typical types include bar charts, box-and-whisker plots and scatterplots.

Histogram: A graphical display of data using bars to represent the frequency of numerical data in defined ranges or intervals. Touching bars indicate continuous data.

Holistic: A holistic approach views human behaviour as a complete, integrated experience, considering the whole person rather than isolating individual components.

Hypothesis: A hypothesis is a specific, testable prediction about the relationship between variables. (Also see 'research question'.)

Independent measures design: An experimental design in which different participants are assigned to each condition. Also known as between-groups design.

Independent variable: The variable manipulated by the researcher to examine its effect on the dependent variable.

Individualism: A cultural orientation that prioritises personal autonomy, independence, and self-expression over group goals and social cohesion. It is often contrasted with collectivism, which emphasises interdependence and group harmony.

Inductive approach: A bottom-up research approach in which theories are developed based on patterns observed in data.

Inferential statistics: Statistical techniques that allow researchers to make inferences or generalisations about a population based on data from a sample.

Inter-coder reliability: The degree of agreement between different researchers coding the same qualitative data, enhancing credibility.

Inter-rater reliability: The consistency of measurements when different people observe or assess the same behaviour.

Internal reliability: How consistently the items in a test or measure assess the same construct.

Internal validity: The extent to which a study establishes a trustworthy cause-and-effect relationship between a treatment and an outcome.

Interpretivist method: A research philosophy that understands human behaviour through subjective analysis, focusing on the meanings individuals attach to their actions. It highlights the importance of personal experiences and cultural context in interpreting behaviour. (Contrast with 'positivist method'.)

Interquartile range (IQR): A measure of statistical dispersion: the difference between the 75th percentile (Q3) and 25th percentile (Q1) values.

Interval data: Data measured along a scale with equal intervals between values but without a true zero point (for example, temperature in degrees Celsius).

Interviewer effect: The influence that the interviewer's characteristics (for example, gender, tone, body language) can have on participant responses.

Interview guide: A structured or semi-structured list of questions or topics used by an interviewer to ensure consistency across participants.

Likert scale: A rating scale on which participants rate how strongly they agree with a statement – for example, from strongly agree to strongly disagree.

Line graph: A chart that displays data points connected by straight lines. It is often used to show trends over time.

Line of best fit: A straight line drawn on a scatterplot to show the general trend displayed by the data.

Longitudinal: A research design that involves repeated observations of the same variables over a long period of time.

Matched pairs design: An experimental design in which participants are paired based on similar characteristics, with one from each pair assigned to a different condition.

Mean: The arithmetic average of a set of values.

Measurement: A key concept exploring the importance of systematically observing and quantifying behaviour or related variables to draw conclusions. Human behaviour is complex; psychologists must carefully select and operationalise methods to ensure reliability and validity.

Measure of central tendency: Statistical measures that describe the centre of a data set: mean, median and mode.

Measure of dispersion: Statistical measures that describe the spread of data: range, interquartile range, standard deviation.

Median: The middle value in a dataset when the numbers are arranged in order.

Member checking: A technique in qualitative research in which participants review and confirm the accuracy of transcripts or findings.

Mode: The most frequently occurring value in a dataset.

Mundane realism: How similar the task and setting are to real-life situations.

Naturalistic observation: Observing subjects in their natural environment without interference or manipulation by the researcher.

Nominal data: Data categorised by name or label without any quantitative value (for example, gender, ethnicity).

Non-parametric test: A statistical test used to analyse data when parametric assumptions are not met (for example, Mann-Whitney, Wilcoxon signed-rank test).

Non-participant observation: Observation in which the researcher does not interact with the participants.

Non-probability sampling: A sampling technique in which not all members of the population have an equal chance of being selected.

Normal distribution: A symmetrical, bell-shaped curve in which most values cluster around the mean and probabilities taper off equally on both sides.

Null hypothesis (H_0): A prediction that there will be no effect or relationship between variables. It is used as a baseline for statistical testing.

Open-ended question: A question that allows for elaborated, unrestricted responses from participants; used in qualitative research.

Operationalise: To define a variable in practical, measurable terms to allow it to be observed and tested in a research study.

Opportunity sampling: A non-random sampling technique in which participants are selected based on convenience or availability.

Ordinal data: Data that represent rank order but does not indicate the exact differences between ranks (for example, 1st, 2nd, 3rd place).

Order effect: A change in participants' performance due to the order in which conditions or tasks are presented (for example, practice or fatigue effects).

Outlier: An extreme value that differs significantly from the rest of the data set.

Overt observation: When participants are aware they are being observed.

Parametric test: A statistical test used to analyse data in which there is a normal distribution and equal variances (for example, t-tests, ANOVA).

Participant observation: A qualitative method in which the researcher actively takes part in the situation being studied while observing behaviours and interactions. Can be overt (participants aware) or covert (unaware).

Participant reactivity: When participants alter their behaviour due to their awareness of being observed in a study.

Participant variability: The differences in characteristics among participants in a study – such as age, gender, intelligence, personality, cultural background or prior experience – that may influence the outcome of the research.

Pearson's *r* test: A statistical measure that assesses the strength and direction of a linear relationship between two variables, ranging from -1 (perfect negative correlation) to +1 (perfect positive correlation).

Perspective: A key concept focusing on how understanding and studying behaviour is based on a set of assumptions about how humans function. Perspectives shape how psychologists develop theories, design research and interpret findings.

Pilot study: A small-scale version of a study conducted to test and refine procedures, measures, and logistics before the full research is carried out.

Pilot test: A preliminary trial of specific components (for example, survey questions) to ensure clarity and effectiveness.

Population of interest (target population): The broader group of individuals the researcher aims to draw conclusions about from their sample.

Population validity: How well the sample represents the broader population.

Positivist method: A research philosophy that assumes reality is objective and can be discovered through scientific measurement and testing. Typically associated with quantitative methods. (Contrast with 'interpretivist method'.)

Practice effect: Improved performance due to repeated exposure to a task, rather than actual treatment effects.

Probability sampling: A sampling method that ensures every member of the population has a known and equal chance of being selected (for example, simple random sampling).

Prolonged engagement: This refers to extended immersion in qualitative research to build trust and credibility.

p-value: The probability of obtaining the observed results, or a more extreme one, if the null hypothesis is true.

Qualitative: Research based on non-numerical data (for example, interviews, observations) that aims to understand meanings, experiences or concepts.

Quantitative: Research based on numerical data, often involving statistical analysis to test hypotheses.

Quasi-experiment: An experiment in which there is no random assignment and groups are organised by pre-existing characteristics.

Questionnaire: A data collection tool that consists of a written set of questions to explore participants' thoughts and experiences.

Random assignment: The process of randomly allocating participants to different experimental conditions to minimise bias.

Random sampling: A technique by which every member of the population has an equal chance of being selected for the sample.

Ratio data: Quantitative data that has equal intervals and a true zero point (for example, height, weight, income).

Recall bias: A type of bias occurring when participants do not accurately remember past events or experiences.

Reductionism: A reductionist approach explains complex behaviour by breaking it down into simpler components, such as biological, cognitive or sociocultural factors. It contrasts with holistic approaches.

Reflexivity: In qualitative research, reflexivity refers to the researcher's awareness of how their own background, values and involvement may affect the research process and interpretation of results.

Reliability: The consistency and dependability of a study or measure.

Repeated measures design: A research design in which the same participants are measured or tested in all conditions.

Representative: A sample that accurately reflects the characteristics of the population from which it is drawn, allowing findings to be generalised.

Research (or alternate) hypothesis (H_1): A statement predicting a relationship or difference between variables, tested against the null hypothesis.

Research question: A research question is a broader inquiry guiding the direction of the study. (Also see 'hypothesis'.)

Responsibility: The ethical obligation of psychologists to respect and protect participants – human or animal – by minimising harm, maximising benefits and applying research in ways that promote social good and avoid misuse or stigma.

Retrospective research: A method that analyses past events, data or records to understand behaviour, relying on historical information and participants' memories.

Sample: A subset of individuals selected from a larger population, intended to represent that population in a research study.

Sampling: Techniques used to select participants for a study, including probability and non-probability methods.

Sampling frame: An accessible group of individuals from which a sample is drawn, representing the population of interest, for example a list or register.

Scatterplot: A graph used to show the relationship between two quantitative variables. Each point represents a pair of values.

Self-report: Where participants provide information about their own thoughts, feelings or behaviours.

Self-selected sampling: A sampling method in which participants volunteer to take part in the study, often by responding to an advertisement or invitation.

Semi-structured interview: An interview format that uses pre-determined questions but allows flexibility for follow-up questions based on participant responses.

Single-blind design: A procedure in which participants do not know whether they are in the experimental or control group, helping to reduce participant bias.

Skewness: A term to describe data that is not symmetrically distributed; it may be positively (right) or negatively (left) skewed.

Snowball sampling: A sampling technique in which existing participants refer or recruit future participants; often used for hard-to-reach populations.

Social desirability bias: The tendency of participants to answer questions in a manner they think will be viewed favourably by others.

Standard deviation (SD): A measure of the spread or dispersion of a set of data points from the mean.

Statistical significance: This is when the likelihood of the results occurring by chance is very low. In psychology, this is typically indicated by a probability level of $p < 0.05$, meaning there is less than a 5 per cent chance that the observed results are due to random variation

Stratified sampling: A probability sampling method in which the population is divided into subgroups (strata) and a random sample is taken from each.

Structured interview: An interview in which all participants are asked the same set of pre-determined questions in the same order.

Structured (systematic) observation: A systematic method of observing and recording behaviour, using a predefined checklist or coding system, often in a controlled setting, to ensure consistency and reliability across observations.

Survey/questionnaire: A survey or questionnaire is a tool used to ask questions of participants on a specific topic. It can be conducted on paper, in person or online. In the context of DP Psychology, the terms are used interchangeably.

Test-retest reliability: A method for assessing the reliability of a measure by comparing results from the same test administered to the same participants after a time interval.

Thematic analysis: A method for identifying, analysing and reporting patterns (themes) within qualitative data.

Thick description: A detailed, in-depth account of research contexts and participants' experiences that helps convey the richness and meaning of data.

Transferability: The extent to which qualitative research findings can be transferred to other contexts or groups. It is similar to generalisability in quantitative research.

Triangulation: A strategy used in research to enhance the credibility and validity of findings by drawing on multiple sources or perspectives. This can include:

- **Data triangulation:** Using data from different times, settings or participants.
- **Method triangulation:** Applying more than one research method to study the same phenomenon.
- **Researcher triangulation:** Involving multiple researchers in data collection or analysis to reduce individual bias.

True experiment: An experiment with random assignment, a control group and manipulation of the independent variable to establish causality.

Type I error: A false positive; rejecting the null hypothesis when it is actually true.

Type II error: A false negative; failing to reject the null hypothesis when it is actually false.

Unstructured interview: A flexible, open-ended interview method in which the interviewer has no fixed set of questions, allowing the researcher to explore topics in depth based on the participant's responses.

Unstructured (unsystematic) observation: A flexible and open-ended method of observing behaviour without predefined categories or checklists, allowing the researcher to record a wide range of behaviours as they occur naturally.

Validity: The extent to which a research study or measurement tool accurately measures what it intends to measure.

Wait-listing: A research design in which some participants receive a treatment later, allowing comparison between those who have received the intervention and those still waiting.

Answers

Chapter 1
Activity 1

1. **a.** self-selected **b.** opportunity **c.** snowball **d.** random **e.** stratified

2. a = University students' sleep habits may be different from the general population, for example later mornings as often not working. Also, university is a more stressful environment with academic pressures, which could limit the generalisability.

   b = Students are required to take PE as part of the IB. They have to engage in activity, which means they may be more active or have higher motivation to exercise than older populations.

   d = Memory may be utilised more often at this age as students are learning new information and retrieving information more regularly, which could affect the results. The type of music students listen to is more likely to be based on popular and current genres, which may not represent all musical styles.

Study in focus: Bandura (1961)

1. Psychological harm: Consent would be needed from the parents as the children are under 16. Debriefing would be necessary to ensure there is no long-lasting harm from imitating the aggression.

2. The study only focused on short-term effects, meaning it is difficult to know whether there was a change in behaviour in the long-term. A follow-up would be needed to examine this further.

3. It would likely face scrutiny today and require additional measures to ensure no long-lasting effects of learning aggression occur.

Chapter 2
Study in focus: Yuki (2003)

1. Strengths: An effective method for collecting large-scale, cross-cultural data, with standardised questions allowing comparisons to be made across cultures. They can gather information on personal beliefs which are not observable.

   Limitations: They lack contextual depth as they do not show actual behaviour, only reported beliefs. As they are often completed independently, especially online surveys, there is a greater chance of misinterpretation of the question, affecting reliability.

2. Participants may feel pressure to answer in a certain way. Social desirability bias can lead participants to give answers that reflect cultural norms rather than actual beliefs. This bias could inflate cultural differences, reducing the validity of the conclusions drawn.

3. Deductive. The research was guided by existing theory – in this case, social identity theory – which predicted differences between Western and East Asian group identity. The survey was designed to test those predictions with a hypothesis, making it theory driven.

Survey design: Reflection

1. The midpoint could be an easy way out of a sensitive topic; it may flatten the data set, and ambiguity requires more follow-up as to why they are neutral.

2. Have follow-up open-ended responses for people to expand, add reflection prompts; the use of these could lead the participants to slow down and reassess their thinking.

Activity 1

1. Mean, median, mode and standard deviation for each factor:

   - Appearance: mean 3.83, median 3.5, mode 5, SD 1.04
   - Shared interests: mean 3.83, median 4, mode 4, SD 0.82
   - Shared values: mean 4.33, median 4, mode 5, SD 0.72
   - Location: mean 4.08, median 4, mode 4, SD 1.18

2. The standard deviation for shared values is 0.72, which suggests relatively low variability in responses. This indicates that participants tended to agree on the importance of shared values when choosing a partner.

3. Outlier identified: Participant 7 rated 'Location' as 1, while most others rated it between 3 and 5. This value is at least two points below the median and may be considered an outlier, suggesting that participant 7 had unusually low concern about geographic proximity.

Activity 2

In total, 16 people answered the neutral point. This could indicate teachers chose not to commit either way.

The number 5 was chosen 24 times, indicating the most frequent, while 1 was chosen the least. This indicates most teachers view positive relationships as important in the classroom.

Activity 3

A frequency table could be used for all of them, before graphing.

1. Line graph to track changes over time (for example, satisfaction across weeks)

2. Scatterplot to explore the relationship between two continuous variables.

3. Box and whisker plot to display the spread, median and outliers in continuous data.

4. Bar graph to compare frequency or average scores across categories.

5. Histogram to show the distribution of continuous data grouped into intervals.

HL Reflection

1. $r = +0.62$ indicates a strong, positive relationship; as social media use increases, conflict increases.

2. Stress or increased workload could lead to increased social media use.

Apply it! Paper 2

1a. The command term 'describe' means you need to give a detailed account of your class practical. For the top band, you need to make sure you explain your aim, sampling technique, how you designed your survey, the procedure and how you analysed it. To get to the top band, you need a clear link between the aim and procedure of a survey and your class practical.

1b. 'Explain' means you need to give a detailed account of how responsibility relates to your survey, either in terms of ways in which you took responsibility or in which further responsibility could be taken. It is good practice to start with a definition. Points which could be made, but are not limited to:

- Protection from harm: How did you ensure the wording was sensitive and not leading? Did you test your questions?

- Anonymity and confidentiality: What measures did you take in trying to ensure the rights of your participants? Why is this important in relation to the topic?

- Consent: Was consent verbal or written? How did you ensure participants did not feel pressured?

Apply it! Paper 3

1. Remember that you only need to provide one issue, but fully explain it. *What is the issue? Why is this an issue? What is the consequence?* HL

Possible responses include, but are not limited to:

- No mention of motivation in the title – although it seems to link to this HL area, there is no explicit mention, with other variables included.

- No sample size given or demographic information – unclear how many students were surveyed or who was in the sample (for example, age). This could affect population validity.

- Lack of operationalisation of the variables – healthy sleep and high academic performance are vague, which could affect the construct validity.

- No error bars to indicate variation – not able to understand variability, which could make the data look more certain than it is.

Chapter 3

Activity 1

1. IV: *Note-taking method*, operationalised as either hand-writing notes with pen and paper or typing notes on a laptop.
   DV: *Memory recall*, operationalised as the number of correct answers on a standardised quiz or test (for example, multiple-choice or short-answer questions) based on the material studied.

2. Null hypothesis (H_0): There will be no significant difference in memory recall between students who hand write their notes and those who type them.

   Directional research hypothesis (H_1): Students who hand write their notes will recall significantly more information than those who type their notes.

   (Alternatively, a non-directional hypothesis could be used: There will be a significant difference in recall between students who hand write and those who type.)

3. Controls include:

- Study content: All participants should take notes on the same material (for example, a passage or lecture).

- Time allowed: The same amount of time should be given to take notes, and these should be tested.

- Test format and timing: Everyone should take the same test, under the same conditions, at the same time after note-taking.

- Prior knowledge: A pre-test or random allocation could be used to control for variation in prior familiarity with the content.

- Typing/writing speed: This could influence the amount of information that is recorded; participants should be pre-screened or matched across conditions.

4. Independent measures design is most suitable as it avoids order effects, prevents participants from guessing the aim and can be completed quickly.

5. True experiment as the researcher can randomly assign participants to conditions and manipulate the IV in a controlled setting.

Study in focus: Tversky and Kahneman (1974)

1. IV: Anchor value – a number introduced before participants make an estimate.
DV: Estimation of the mathematical problem.

2. Independent measures: Participants took part in only one condition.

Study in focus: Loftus and Palmer (1974)

1. Any two from:

- Standardisation: All participants watched the same set of video clips of car accidents and were asked similarly structured questions with only the verb manipulated.

- Timing: All participants were questioned immediately after viewing the clips to ensure consistency in memory recall timing.

- Materials: The same number of videos were watched.

2. A video of a real accident may have caused distress.

3. A video of a crash does not evoke the same intensity and emotional reaction as witnessing a real-life car accident; this questions the mundane realism.

Study in focus: Maguire et al. (2000)

1. The independent variable (taxi-driver status) already existed; participants were not randomly allocated to become a taxi driver or a control. Because this grouping factor was pre-existing, it was a quasi-experiment rather than a true experiment.

2. Without random assignment, confounding variables (such as innate spatial ability, stress, lifestyle) may have explained any differences found in hippocampal volume. The relationship between the number of years driving and hippocampal volume was also only correlational, so cause-and-effect cannot be established. Therefore, it cannot be definitively claimed that taxi driving causes hippocampal growth.

Activity 2

1. No. The p-value is 0.08, which is greater than the significance level of 0.05, so the result is not statistically significant. The null hypothesis should be accepted.

2. With only eight participants per group, the study has low statistical power, making it harder to detect small-to-moderate effects. This increases the likelihood of a type II error. A type II error occurs when we fail to reject a false null hypothesis. It's possible that caffeine may improve memory, but the study didn't detect it. The mean for the caffeine group (13.6) is noticeably higher than the placebo group (11.25). This could be due to the small sample size.

Apply It! Paper 2

1a. The command term 'describe' means you need to give a detailed account of your class practical. For the top band, you need to ensure that you explain your aim, hypothesis, sampling technique, experiment design and procedure. To get to the top band, you need to show detailed knowledge and understanding of an experiment as used in your class practical

1b. 'Explain' means you need to give a detailed account of how measurement relates to your experiment. This could be how you planned your practical, for example defining variables. You should provide answers to the following questions to answer Question 1b.

- How did you operationalise your independent and dependent variables. Why did these operational definitions capture the constructs you aimed to study?

- How are these operational definitions reflected in your research and null hypotheses?
- How did you establish construct validity for your measures?
- Why did you select (or design) the specific tool or scale for your dependent variable? To what extent did the tool measure what you intended to measure?

1c. Both experiments and observations use standardised procedures, such as pre-defined operational definitions, timing and recording sheets, to ensure consistent data collection and replication. Both methods can be carried out in laboratory or naturalistic settings, depending on whether the research prioritises control or ecological validity. Additionally, both methods can produce quantitative data – such as measuring the frequency or duration of behaviours – making them suitable for identifying patterns and comparing across conditions or participants.

Experiments, however, manipulate an independent variable while holding extraneous variables constant, allowing researchers to infer causal relationships. Observations merely record naturally occurring behaviour. This means they can identify correlations or trends, but cannot establish cause and effect. Furthermore, experiments are often conducted in artificial environments that may reduce ecological validity, whereas observations typically take place in real-world settings, increasing the realism and generalisability of the findings, but at the cost of reduced control and possible observer bias.

HL ## Apply It! Paper 3

2. The results show that students in the intervention group (Group A), who used the mindfulness app, reported higher well-being scores after the three-week period compared to the control group (Group B). As it was a matched pairs design, the median scores for well-being are similar. However, after three weeks, Group A's median score increased from 39 to 53, while Group B's median remained virtually unchanged (39 to 40). This suggests a strong effect of app use on improving well-being. However, the increase in Group A's interquartile range (IQR) suggests that greater variability between participants.

The box plot in **Figure 1** visually supports the impact of the mindfulness app, showing the extent of the changes. There is no overlap between the IQRs of Group A and Group B, indicating a clear difference between the groups. It can be seen that some participants' well-being score decreased in Group B, further supporting the idea that the app had a protective or enhancing effect.

Since the study used a randomised controlled trial with matched pairs, the findings are likely due to the effect of the mindfulness app, rather than chance or confounding variables. These results support the claim that health and well-being apps can effectively improve student well-being, especially when used regularly over time.

Chapter 4

Study in focus: Lueck and Wilson (2010)

1. By using a semi-structured interview to explore sensitive or complex issues around acculturative stress, the researchers were able to adapt the questions based on the participants' responses. As acculturative stress is unique to an individual, it is important that the researcher can ask follow-up questions, probe further and go beyond the interview schedule. The conversational style allows a rapport to build and participants to be more open about their experiences.

2. Having an interviewer who shared a similar cultural or social background with participants helped reduce potential bias by fostering trust and mutual understanding. This likely minimised response distortion, as participants felt more comfortable being open and honest. It allowed participants to feel at ease, which reduced social desirability bias. Additionally, cultural alignment between interviewer and participant reduced the likelihood of misinterpretation of responses, improving the authenticity of the data collected.

3. To enhance credibility, the researchers used multiple strategies such as member checks (participants reviewed the findings for accuracy), researcher triangulation (multiple researchers interpreted the data) and prolonged engagement, with interviews lasting approximately 2.4 hours. Additionally, interview transcripts were translated and back translated to maintain linguistic accuracy and conceptual consistency, ensuring meaning was not lost in analysis.

4. Informed consent: It is important that participants are fully informed about the personal nature of the topic, to allow them to feel comfortable participating. They should be made aware they can withdraw at any time, including after the interview. They should also be informed that their data will remain anonymous, and that the data will only be used for the study.

Protection from harm: When dealing with sensitive or potentially distressing topics, researchers should ensure participants feel safe and supported throughout the interview process. Researchers should be ready to offer resources or support through their debrief if participants get upset discussing their personal experiences.

Study in focus: Brown and Harris (1978)

Strengths	
Flexibility: Interviewers can adapt questions and probe deeper based on participant responses, allowing exploration of sensitive or unexpected issues.	Brown and Harris used flexible interviews to explore how life events and social support influenced depression, tailoring questions to each woman's experience.
Rich data: Produces detailed, qualitative information that gives insight into complex psychological and social factors.	The researchers collected in-depth life histories that revealed patterns of vulnerability (for example, loss, lack of support) linked to depression.
Rapport: Building trust encourages openness and honesty, especially on personal topics like mental health.	Participants were more willing to share emotional and potentially stigmatised experiences due to the empathetic, conversational format of the interviews.
Limitations	
Time consuming: Semi-structured interviews take a long time to conduct, transcribe and analyse, especially in large samples.	Brown and Harris conducted over 400 interviews, which required significant time and resources.
Interviewer bias: Interviewers may unintentionally influence responses through their tone, phrasing or interpretation.	The subjective nature of coding life events may have introduced researcher bias into the categorisation of vulnerability factors.
Need for trained interviewers: Skilled interviewers are essential to manage sensitive topics effectively and reduce bias.	Brown and Harris relied on trained professionals to explore emotional topics without causing distress or influencing responses.

Activity 1

1. Structural question
2. Descriptive question
3. Evaluative question
4. Contrast question

Bonus: Student's own answer

Activity 2

1. Yes, this is a common topic discussed in focus groups. However, it depends on the level of stress being discussed and whether a one-to-one interview would be better. A questionnaire/survey would also work well.

2. Yes, this would form the basis of a focus group discussion.

3. No. A group setting may make individuals conform to peer pressure within the group. A one-to-one interview may be better for this topic. Also, there may be social desirability – students may not respond truthfully with peers present.

4. No. A one-to-one interview would be best given the very personal nature of the topic. Anonymity would be hard to establish and maintain in a group setting.

5. Yes, a focus group could be a useful method. If students are from the same time, participants may be more willing to share answers. However, existing dynamics may affect participation. Therefore, the researcher would need to consider how to control for dominant responder bias. An experiment could also be done.

Activity 3

Answers will vary depending on your transcript.

Apply It! Paper 2

1a. For the full 4 marks, you need to clearly explain how you undertook the interview or focus group for your class practical and apply correct terminology. This could include how you obtained your sample, the tools used (for example, interview guide), how you recorded the interview and any ethical considerations.

1b. 1b. 'Explain' means you need to give a detailed account of how bias relates to your interview or focus group, either in terms of the ways you reduced bias or further biases that could be present. It is good practice to start with a definition. Points which could be made, but are not limited to:

- Sampling bias: Consider how the sampling technique may have influenced the findings – for example, the use of non-probability sampling techniques often used in qualitative research.

- Interviewer bias: Preconceived ideas based on their background, as students may bring bias into their research, affecting their tone, body language or informal cues, which could affect understanding.

- Social desirability can arise when participants give answers to please the researcher.

- Confirmation bias may arise in semi-structured interviews if the researcher intentionally pursues a specific line of questioning and ignores other responses due to pre-existing beliefs.

- Recall bias: Participants may not accurately remember past events, thoughts or behaviours.

1c. You should write two well-developed paragraphs explaining similarities (compare) and differences (contrast) in detail. You must use psychological terminology relevant to interviews and experiments effectively. Use sentence starters such as 'One similarity between interviews and experiments is that they both…' and 'A key difference is that interviews… while experiments…'. Use the comparison table in Chapter 3 to remind yourself of key similarities and differences between the two.

1d. When designing an alternative, it is important that you do not change the aim of your original class practical. The procedure needs to be explained with accuracy and detail. Psychological terminology relating to surveys must be used effectively.

Apply It! Paper 3

3. You need to include a definition of credibility at the start, for example: *Credibility refers to the extent to which the findings of a qualitative study can be trusted as an accurate reflection of the participants' experiences.*

Points could include:

- Sampling bias: Only eight students, which limits generalisability to other IB students; a wider sample could be obtained.

- Recall bias: Reliant on self-reporting that students watched the video; not able to verify they did watch the video.

- Dominant responder bias: One member of the group could dominate the discussion, which could skew findings. An anonymous form of data collection could also be used to capture all voices.

- Method triangulation: Participants may not feel comfortable sharing in front of peers or there could be social desirability. Therefore, the researcher could combine surveys, focus groups and app usage data.

- Researcher triangulation: This can verify their themes are trustworthy, improving the inter-rater reliability.

- Member checking: Referencing the identified themes.

- Reflexivity: Own beliefs about mindfulness and digital tools plus a reflexivity journal.

Refer to section 1.3 in Chapter 1 to see the mark scheme.

Here is an example response:

Credibility refers to the extent to which the findings of a qualitative study can be trusted as an accurate reflection of the participants' experiences.

One way in which the researcher could improve credibility is through method triangulation. In the focus group, some participants may not have felt comfortable discussing their experiences of mindfulness with their peers due to the personal nature of the topic. In addition, social desirability may inflate self-reported usage. By comparing the app's automatic usage logs, results from an anonymous online usage survey and the focus group transcripts, the researcher can check whether the themes align with actual practice.

Credibility could be improved through reflexivity. The researcher should acknowledge how their own mindfulness practice, employment by the app developer or student-teacher relationships may influence questioning or interpretation. A reflexive diary and discussing entries with a peer, would encourage critical self-reflection and reduce the likelihood of confirmation bias.

Finally, member checking can validate the thematic analysis. The researcher could ask participants whether the themes identified align with their experiences as a way to validate the data. For example, whether 'mindfulness makes them feel calmer' is accurate or whether a different adjective would summarise their feelings. If participants confirm or refine the wording, the data becomes more trustworthy.

With triangulation, reflexive practice and member checking in place, the study's findings would be much more credible.

Chapter 5

Study in focus: Fagot (1978)

1. The follow-up survey corroborates the observational findings, which increases the credibility of the results because two independent methods converge on the same pattern of parental feedback.

2. Informed consent: Parents were the primary participants giving consent, but the young children being observed could not provide fully informed consent. *Safeguard*: Ensure that parental consent is obtained for all observations, and explain the purpose of the study in age-appropriate terms to older children when possible.

   Privacy and confidentiality: The study was conducted in family homes, a private setting, which raises concerns about the protection of personal information. *Safeguard: Observational data should be anonymised, and no identifiable information (such as names, recordings) should be disclosed or published.*

   Right to withdraw: Participants may feel uncomfortable withdrawing once the observation begins, especially in a home setting. *Safeguard: Clearly inform families at the outset that they may withdraw from the study at any time without consequences. Remind them of this right throughout the study.*

Reflection

Five behaviours:

1. On-task non-verbal – pointing, nodding or placing puzzle pieces without talking
2. On-task verbal – verbal discussion about the given puzzle
3. Non-verbal engagement – sustained eye contact with puzzle or partner for more than 3 seconds
4. Off-task talking – conversation unrelated to the puzzle
5. Off-task behaviour – leaving seat, phone use, fidgeting unrelated to the task

Activity 1

1. Structured, naturalistic, overt, non-participant observation: Uses a checklist of predefined behaviours (structured). It takes place in a real-world early childhood setting (naturalistic). Permission from parents and school (overt), and the researcher does not interact with the children (non-participant).

2. Unstructured, naturalistic, covert, non-participant observation: Uses open-ended field notes, not a predefined checklist (unstructured). A café is a public setting (naturalistic). The teenagers are unaware of being observed (covert) and the student does not interact (non-participant).

3. Unstructured, naturalistic, covert, participant observation: The psychologist makes mental notes without a checklist (unstructured). The setting is a real early childhood environment (naturalistic). Children are unaware of the observation (covert), and the researcher joins the play (participant).

4. Structured, controlled, overt, non-participant observation: The psychologist uses a tally system with predefined behaviours (structured). The play setting is pre-designed and observed through a two-way mirror (controlled). Parents will have consented (overt), and the researcher does not engage in the behaviour (non-participant).

Activity 2

Scenario	Best graph or table	Reason for choice
Scenario 1 – Frequency of three play categories	Bar graph	Categorical, discreet counts. Bars make it easy to compare across categories.

Scenario	Best graph or table	Reason for choice
Scenario 2 – Minutes each student stays on task	Box and whisker plot	Duration is continuous. A box and whisker plot shows median, quartiles and any outliers clearly. A histogram is also acceptable but gives less summary information for a quick comparison.
Scenario 3 – Two continuous measures per student	Scatterplot	To show the correlation between two variables.
Scenario 4 – Count of five distinct behaviours in a group project	Bar graph	Categorical frequencies.

Activity 3

- Small, age-specific sample: The study only observed 4–5-year-olds. Findings may not transfer to older children or adolescents, who regulate emotions differently.

- Single cultural and environmental context: All children attended the same suburban centre. Results may not reflect behaviour in rural, urban or culturally diverse settings.

- Natural setting improves ecological validity: The use of an authentic free-play environment increases the likelihood that behaviour observed reflects real-world interactions.

- Unstructured observation allows rich insight: Detailed field notes may capture subtle behaviours and context, making findings useful for similar early childhood educators or researchers.

- Limited generalisability: The subjective nature of unstructured observation and reliance on one researcher's interpretation may reduce transferability unless detailed descriptions are provided.

- Transferability depends on thick descriptions: Others can assess whether the context (for example, age, setting, play structure) matches their own, but the researcher must provide thorough reporting for this to happen.

Apply it! Paper 2

Refer to Chapter 1 to see the mark scheme for Section B. Here is a model response.

This study can be critically discussed in terms of causality, measurement and bias.

The use of a true experiment with random assignment supports a strong causal inference. By manipulating the independent variable (study strategy) and controlling the learning materials and time allocated, the researchers aimed to isolate the effect of the type of practice (independent variable) on memory recall (dependent variable). The significant result strengthens this claim. However, the one-week delay introduces potential confounding variables that could weaken internal validity, such as unmonitored rehearsal, or conversation between participants. Individual differences in prior knowledge and intrinsic motivation could also have influenced recall. Counterbalancing the articles or adding a baseline prior-knowledge test would have reduced these threats to internal validity.

When discussing measurement, the one-week delay between learning and testing aligns the dependent variable with long-term rather than short-term memory, which strengthens construct validity. However, the 10-item factual recall test assesses surface knowledge only; adding a conceptual question or free-recall section would capture deeper retention. Moreover, reliability is uncertain as the scoring procedure and blinding are not described. Using a standard mark scheme and double-scoring the answers would improve the inter-rater reliability.

Sampling bias limits the generalisability of the findings. The sample consisted of high school students from one school, which may not reflect wider student populations. The retrieval group may have anticipated the follow-up test, producing an expectancy effect. Blinding the participants to the true aim and administering an unrelated filler task could reduce this bias. Two researchers analysing the data could help reduce confirmation bias, but only if both independently scored the recall tests and followed the same marking criteria and were blind to group allocation. The report omits these details.

In conclusion, while the study provides moderate support for a causal link between retrieval practice and improved long-term memory, limitations in measurement and potential sampling bias reduce the generalisability of the findings. Future research should use more diverse samples, multi-dimensional memory tests and stronger blinding procedures to strengthen the causal claim.

Apply it! Paper 3

Refer to Chapter 1 to see the mark scheme for Paper 3 Question 4 and what you need to do to reach the top mark band. Here are some key points that you should have included in your answer.

You need to use **at least three sources** in support of their evaluation:

- Source 2: An experimental study with a pre/post-test design, showing improved well-being scores after a three-week mindfulness app intervention. Supports causal interpretation, but only one health and well-being app type tested longer-term use compared to the other sources.

- Source 3: A focus group that reports short-term subjective benefits (calmness, mental clarity) after mindfulness app use. However, this was self-reported, with a very small sample size.

- Source 4: A correlational study reporting a positive correlation ($r = 0.35$) between app usage frequency and well-being, supporting the claim. However, no causal inference can be made. Self-selection bias: more motivated or mentally healthy students may use apps more; did not sample those who did not use apps already.

- Source 5: Reports on objective data from a well-being tracking app and highlights differences across app types (for example, mindfulness vs sleep vs journalling), finding a correlation. However, there was no clear pre/post comparison, or use of a control group. Does not differentiate between active and passive use.

Discussion points: A strong response will engage critically with the claim and sources, addressing conceptual and methodological issues.

Possible discussion points include:

- Operationalisation of well-being: Vague or inconsistent definitions – for example, mood, sleep, energy, stress. Use of standardised tools increases construct validity (WEMWBS, WHO-Five Well-Being Index, PSS).

- Variation across app types: Fitness, mindfulness and journalling apps may differ in effect; however, studies often group them together, reducing construct validity.

- Limitations of self-report data: Many studies rely on self-reported app use and well-being outcomes. This is prone to recall bias and social desirability.

- Causality and research design: Most evidence is correlational. Source 2 is experimental, but short-term and limited in scope.

- Sample characteristics and generalisability: Most studies are on university students or volunteer sampling. Lacks generalisability to younger students or broader populations.

- Short-term vs long-term effects: Few studies assess whether benefits are sustained over time. Longitudinal data is needed in the area.

- Confounding and motivational factors: There are variables not considered in the sources. For example, students who use apps regularly may also engage in other well-being behaviours. Self-selection bias must be considered.

- Ethical and technological considerations: Apps collect sensitive data. Are they trustworthy? Are they evidence-based or commercially driven?

- Lack of comparison to offline interventions: No source compares well-being apps to traditional interventions (therapy, in-person mindfulness), which may lead findings to be prone to confirmation bias.

- Cultural bias: Most apps are designed with Western concepts of well-being (for example, individualistic mindfulness), which may not be appropriate or effective for students from collectivist or non-Western cultures.

- Use of research: Relevant research from the HL area can be applied.

Chapter 6

Activity

1. A Likert-scale questionnaire with at least five items, measuring self-esteem and frequency of social media use. Surveys collect data efficiently and allow for quick analysis.

   Challenge: Social desirability bias leading to inaccurate self-reporting

2. A semi-structured interview guide with more than five open-ended questions. Allows for rich, personal data and flexibility to explore unexpected themes.

   Challenge: Interviewer bias, leading questions or participants withholding sensitive information

3. An observation checklist with clearly defined behavioural categories (for example, offers help). Allows for systematic and consistent recording of observable behaviour.

   Challenge: Observer bias or difficulty identifying reasons behind behaviours

References

Chapter 1

Bandura, A., Ross, D, and Ross, S. A. (1961). Transmission of aggression through imitation of aggressive models. *The Journal of Abnormal and Social Psychology, 63*(3), 575–582. https://doi.org/10.1037/h0045925

Chapter 2

Yuki, M. (2003). Intergroup comparison versus intragroup relationships: A cross-cultural examination of social identity theory in North American and East Asian cultural contexts. *Social Psychology Quarterly, 66*(2), 166–183. https://doi.org/10.2307/1519846

Chapter 3

Bandura, A., Ross, D, and Ross, S. A. (1961). Transmission of aggression through imitation of aggressive models. *The Journal of Abnormal and Social Psychology, 63*(3), 575–582. https://doi.org/10.1037/h0045925

Loftus, E. F. and Palmer, J. C. (1974). Reconstruction of automobile destruction: An example of the interaction between language and memory. *Journal of Verbal Learning and Verbal Behavior, 13*(5), 585–589. https://doi.org/10.1016/S0022-5371(74)80011-3

Maguire, E. A., Gadian, D. G., Johnsrude, I. S., Good, C. D., Ashburner, J., Frackowiak, R. S. and Frith, C. D. (2000). Navigation-related structural change in the hippocampi of taxi drivers. *Proceedings of the National Academy of Sciences, 97*(8), 4398–4403. https://doi.org/10.1073/pnas.070039597 (2000).

Tversky, A. and Kahneman, D. (1974) Judgment under uncertainty: Heuristics and Biases. *Science*, 185, 1124-1131. https://doi.org/10.1126/science.185.4157.1124

Chapter 4

Braun, V. and Clarke, V. (2006). Using thematic analysis in psychology. *Qualitative Research in Psychology, 3*(2), 77–101. https://doi.org/10.1191/1478088706qp063oa

Brown, G. W. and Harris, T. (1978). *Social origins of depression: A study of psychiatric disorder in women.* London: Tavistock Publications; New York: Free Press.

Lueck, K. and Wilson, M. (2010). Acculturative stress in Asian immigrants: The impact of social and linguistic factors. *International Journal of Intercultural Relations, 34*(1), 47–57. https://doi.org/10.1016/j.ijintrel.2009.10.004

Chapter 5

Ainsworth, M. D. S., Blehar, M. C., Waters, E. and Wall, S. (1978). Patterns of attachment: A psychological study of the strange situation. Lawrence Erlbaum.

Fagot, B. I. (1978). The influence of sex of child on parental reactions to toddler children. *Child Development, 49*(2), 459–465. https://doi.org/10.2307/1128711

Chapter 6

Baddeley, A. D. and Hitch, G. (1974). Working memory. *Psychology of Learning and Motivation*, 8, 47–89. http://doi.org/10.1016/S0079-7421(08)60452-1

Dunlosky, J., Rawson, K. A., Marsh, E. J., Nathan, M. J., and Willingham, D. T. (2013). Improving students' *learning with effective learning* techniques: Promising directions from cognitive and educational psychology. Psychological Science in the Public Interest, 14(1), 4–58. https://doi.org/10.1177/1529100612453266

Perham, N. *and Vizard, J. (2011). Can preference for back*ground music mediate the irrelevant sound effect? Applied Cognitive Psychology, 25(4), 625–631. https://doi.org/10.1002/acp.1731

Salamé, P. and Baddeley, A. D. (1982). Disruption of short-term memory by unattended speech: Implications for the structure of working memory. Journal *of Verbal Learning & Verbal Behavior, 21(2), 150*–164. https://doi.org/10.1016/S0022-5371(82)90521-7

Index